Henry Brougham Loch

Personal Narrative of Occurrences during Lord Elgin's second

Embassy to China, 1860

Henry Brougham Loch

Personal Narrative of Occurrences during Lord Elgin's second Embassy to China, 1860

ISBN/EAN: 9783337166960

Printed in Europe, USA, Canada, Australia, Japan

Cover: Foto ©Andreas Hilbeck / pixelio.de

More available books at **www.hansebooks.com**

EARL OF ELGIN'S
SECOND EMBASSY TO CHINA.

HENRY BROUGHAM LOCH,

From a Painting by the late Henry W. Phillips.

PERSONAL NARRATIVE

OF OCCURRENCES DURING LORD ELGIN'S

SECOND EMBASSY TO CHINA, 1860.

By HENRY BROUGHAM LOCH,
PRIVATE SECRETARY TO THE EARL OF ELGIN.

PAH-LI-CHIOU BRIDGE.

LONDON:
JOHN MURRAY, ALBEMARLE STREET.
1869.

LONDON:
BRADBURY, EVANS, AND CO., PRINTERS, WHITEFRIARS.

CONTENTS.

CHAPTER I.
CIRCUMSTANCES THAT LED TO LORD ELGIN'S SECOND EMBASSY TO CHINA 1

CHAPTER II.
LORD ELGIN'S DEPARTURE FOR CHINA.—POSITION OF AFFAIRS, AND COURSE OF ACTION ADOPTED ON HIS ARRIVAL IN THAT COUNTRY 11

CHAPTER III.
LANDING AT PEH-TANG 38

CHAPTER IV.
STEPS TAKEN TO OBTAIN INFORMATION OF ENEMY'S POSITION 49

CHAPTER V.
DESCRIPTION OF THE POSITION OF THE NORTHERN AND TAKU FORTS. 57

CHAPTER VI.
CAPTURE OF SINHO 64

CHAPTER VII.
CORRESPONDENCE OF LORD ELGIN AND THE GOVERNOR-GENERAL OF CHIH-LI 74

CHAPTER VIII.
CAPTURE OF THE NORTH TAKU FORTS 80

CHAPTER IX.
ADVANCE TO TIEN-TSIN 112

CHAPTER X.

MARCH TOWARDS **PEKIN.**—**NEGOTIATIONS.**—TREACHERY TO FLAG OF **TRUCE.**—**CAPTURE OF** MESSRS. PARKES, DE NORMANN, LIEUT. ANDERSON, BOWLBY, PHIPPS OF THE K. D. G., THE **SIKH** ESCORT, MYSELF 127

CHAPTER XI.

MY PRISON LIFE 176

CHAPTER XII.

OUR PRISON LIFE . . . 197

CHAPTER XIII.

PROCEEDINGS OF THE **ALLIED** ARMIES FROM THE 18TH SEPTEMBER,—THE **DAY OF OUR** CAPTURE, TO THE 8TH **OF OCTOBER,**—THE **DAY OF** OUR RELEASE . . 239

CHAPTER XIV.

SURRENDER OF **THE BODIES OF MESSRS.** DE NORMANN, ANDERSON, BOWLBY, PHIPPS, AND THOSE **OF** NINE SIKHS, TOGETHER WITH THE RETURN OF TEN SIKHS **AND** THREE FRENCH SOLDIERS,—SURVIVORS.—NEGOTIATIONS 252

CHAPTER XV.

YUEN-MING-YUEN.—A SECOND VISIT TO PEKIN . . 268

CHAPTER XVI.

SIGNATURE OF CONVENTION.—RETURN TO ENGLAND.—FUTURE **POLICY TO BE PURSUED TOWARDS CHINA** . 282

LIST OF ILLUSTRATIONS.

PORTRAIT OF AUTHOR	*Frontispiece.*
PAH-LI-CHIOU BRIDGE . . .	*Title-page.*
INSIDE OF THE TAKU FORT . .	*Page* 86
MAP . . .	*At the end.*

PERSONAL NARRATIVE,

ETC.

CHAPTER I.

CIRCUMSTANCES THAT LED TO LORD ELGIN'S SECOND EMBASSY TO CHINA.

YEARS have passed since the events I am about to describe took place, and although the same interest with which they were invested at the period of their occurrence has passed away, I venture to believe there will be still some who will read with interest a short account of a very eventful period of Chinese history, when Lord Elgin, breaking through the old traditional policy of China, established on a new basis our intercourse with that country, which was afterwards ably fostered and matured by Sir Frederick Bruce.

The following narrative pretends to be no

more than a few extracts from my Diary; it has no pretension to being a complete history or an official record of Lord Elgin's second Embassy, and to avoid any reference to matters likely to lead to discussion of a controversial character, I have endeavoured to confine myself almost exclusively to the description of those events which came under my personal observation.

Mr. Oliphant wrote such an able account of Lord Elgin's first Embassy that it has increased the hesitation with which I approach the task I have imposed on myself.

To render what I am about to relate intelligible to the general reader, I must go back to the period that immediately succeeded the conclusion of the Treaty of Tientsin, in August, 1858, which we then believed and hoped was the final settlement of the Chinese difficulties which had grown out of the seizure of the lorcha "Arrow" at Canton, in 1856.

Sir Frederick, then Mr. Bruce, secretary to Lord Elgin's Embassy, brought the Treaty to England, and shortly after his arrival he was appointed Her Majesty's Envoy and Minister Plenipotentiary in China, with instructions to return to that country and to exchange the ratifications of the treaty at Pekin. Mr. Bruce's departure from England was somewhat delayed, as the Government were anxious that his instructions might be framed after consultation with Lord Elgin, whose immediate return was at that time anticipated; but when the Government learnt that Lord Elgin, after his successful negotiation of the Treaty of Yeddo, had, for the purpose of ascertaining the real state of the rebellion in the centre of China, gone up the Yang-tze-Kiang, Mr. Bruce was at once ordered to proceed to his post. At Singapore, however, he met Lord Elgin, then on his way home, and thus fortunately had an opportunity of discussing the steps he proposed to take on his arrival in China.

After concerting measures at Hong Kong with Admiral Hope and Sir Charles Straubenzee, that he was to be supported by a strong demonstration of force at the mouth of the Peiho river, Mr. Bruce proceeded to Shanghai, where he arrived on the 6th of June, 1859; M. de Bourboulon, the minister appointed by the Emperor Napoleon to exchange the ratification of the

French treaty at Pekin, arriving the following day.

The two ministers found waiting their arrival at Shanghai, a communication from Kweiliang, one of the commissioners who had the previous year negotiated the Treaty of Tien-tsin, endeavouring to divert them from their purpose of proceeding to Pekin; but he was at once given clearly to understand that the resolution of the ambassadors to proceed there was inflexible, and Mr. Ward, the United States minister, likewise expressed his determination to exchange the ratification of the treaty which had been concluded between China and his country in the capital of the Empire, and to claim an interview with the Emperor.

On the 15th of June Mr. Bruce sailed for the Peiho, and arrived off that river on the 20th of the same month. Admiral Hope had already crossed the bar with several gun-boats. He found, however, the river obstructed by rafts moored across the entrance; but as he had failed in his attempt to open communication with any mandarin, he had been unable to ascertain whether the symptoms of an intended resistance to the admission into the river of a gunboat to convey Mr. Bruce to Tien-tsin, was by order of the Imperial Government, or an act of the local authorities. The men who garrisoned the forts hoisted no flag, and represented themselves to be militia and country people, who had erected the defences to protect themselves from piratical attack, and stated they were acting without authority from Pekin. At first they expressed their readiness to remove the barriers, so as to admit of the passage of one gunboat; but failed to fulfil their promise, and subsequently denied having made it.

As the 26th of June was the date by which, according to the treaty, the ratification had to be exchanged, Mr. Bruce felt, if it was allowed to pass without that ceremony being completed, it was probable the Chinese would take advantage of the circumstance to attempt a re-discussion of those clauses, to which they had more especially objected when the treaty had been concluded the previous year; and therefore, in conjunction with his French colleague, he decided on taking such steps as lay in his power to reach Pekin by the day named.

The absence of any official mandarin at the Peiho, and the persistence of the garrison in saying that they were acting on their own account, prevented Mr. Bruce from assuming that the obstruction of the river was a hostile act on the part of the Imperial Government; and he therefore requested the Admiral to take the necessary measures for removing the rafts, &c., that had been moored across the river, so that he might proceed at once to Tien-tsin, on his way to Pekin.

The attack on the forts, and the disastrous repulse, was the result.

Mr. Bruce, with M. de Bourboulon, returned to Shanghai to wait instructions from Europe, and Admiral Hope withdrew to refit his squadron.

From the comparative ease with which the same forts had been captured the previous year, and from past experience of Chinese warfare, neither the Admiral nor Mr. Bruce could have anticipated the possibility of failure with the powerful naval force at their command, and the information that has since been acquired respecting the feelings which at that time influenced the conduct of the Chinese Government fully justified the policy pursued by Mr. Bruce.

Had the attempt to force the passage of the Peiho been attended with success, it is probable the Emperor would have denied all participation in the effort at resistance, and received Mr. Bruce with all the courtesy and honour due to his position. This view of the case is further strengthened by the fact, that while the preparations were in progress for resistance at Taku, a house was prepared for Mr. Bruce's reception at Pekin.

The success, however, that had attended the defence of the entrance to the river enabled the war party to acquire increased influence, and the Emperor, even if his policy had been pacific, would have been powerless to stem the strong feeling that was aroused by what, not only in the eyes of the Chinese but in that of European countries, could only be viewed as a great military success; and Sang-ko-lin-sin, a Mongol Prince and head of the war party, who, by his successful defence of Tien-tsin against the rebels in 1853 had acquired great renown and influence, seized the opportunity for urging his long-cherished hope of driving into the sea the "Barbarians" who had for so many years dared to insult and dictate terms to the Celestial Empire.

On the arrival in England of the news of the Peiho disaster, the Government decided, in concert with that of the Emperor Napoleon, that a large combined force should be sent to the north of China, to enforce an apology from the Imperial Government, and to ensure a proper and faithful observance for the future of the Treaty of Tien-tsin. But while the Government was supported by the general voice of the country in their determination to act with requisite vigour, a strong feeling existed that if such an extensive war was to be undertaken, the efforts of diplomacy, backed by the presence of a strong fleet and army, ought first to be exhausted before all hope of a pacific solution of the question was abandoned.

The fleet was strengthened by despatch-vessels and gunboats sent from England, and Admiral Jones was appointed second in command to Admiral Hope. An army was organised in India, the command of which was given to Lieutenant-General Sir Hope Grant, whose distinguished services during the Indian Mutiny, and his previous knowledge of China, where he had served as Brigade-Major to Lord Saltoun, made his appointment to be regarded with general satisfaction.

Early in March, 1860, Lord John Russell announced in the House of Commons, that Lord Elgin had accepted the post of Ambassador to the Court of Pekin, and would proceed immediately to China.

It is not easy to appreciate to the full extent the difficulties of the task which Lord Elgin was called on to undertake; but his former experience and great success had imparted such confidence at home in his sound judgment and discretion, that there was almost an unanimous expression of opinion that if, after what had occurred at the Peiho, any satisfactory terms could be arranged with the Chinese Government, which would obviate the necessity of embarking in a war, the duration and results of which could not be foreseen, the best hope of success lay in Lord Elgin's immediate return to China ; and at the same time, if coercive measures became necessary, it was felt that, while he would urge their prosecution with vigour, it would be for only so long as might be requisite to secure the terms which the sense of the country, for future security, demanded.

Baron Gros, with whom Lord Elgin had acted with so much success and pleasure in his first Embassy to China, was also re-appointed as the Emperor Napoleon's representative at the Court of Pekin.

CHAPTER II.

LORD ELGIN'S DEPARTURE FOR CHINA.—POSITION OF AFFAIRS, AND COURSE OF ACTION ADOPTED ON HIS ARRIVAL IN THAT COUNTRY.

On the 26th of April, 1860, three years, to a day, since he started on his first Embassy to China, Lord Elgin left London, and on the 28th embarked at Marseilles on board the P. and O. steamer "Valetta," Capt. Roberts. The Embassy consisted of Colonel Crealock, military secretary; Hon. J. F. Stuart Wortley, and the Hon. T. J. Hovell Thurlow, attachés; and myself, as private secretary. Baron Gros embarked at the same time, accompanied by M. Bastard.

On the 4th of May we arrived at Alexandria. The Pasha placed his palaces and carriages at Lord Elgin's disposal, but we proceeded straight to Cairo, and preferred going to the hotel. Embarked at Suez on the 5th, and arrived at Point de Galle on the 21st. There we were unfortunately detained a fortnight by the wreck of the "Malabar," the steamer that was to have taken us on to China. We had embarked about one o'clock, expecting to proceed to sea in an hour's time; but the severe weather which ushers in the change of the monsoon at this season had delayed the shipment of the cargo by the time expected. The harbour being open to the heavy rollers of the southwest monsoon, the ship pitched heavily as the seas came rolling past; she was hove short ready for starting, with a hawser at the stern, when without any warning the monsoon flew round to the north-east, took the steamer on her broadside, the warp parted, and she tailed on to some rocks, and in a few minutes her stern was stove in. Steam was got up as rapidly as possible, and the captain tried by steaming ahead to set the steam pumps to work; it, however, was too late, the water was up to the deck of the saloon, and momentarily threatened to burst the bulk-head into the engine room. Captain Grainger then decided to try to beach her at the head of the harbour to avoid sinking in deep water, but she was now so water-logged she was nearly unmanageable. Owing to this and the tremendous sea that was running, it was with much difficulty her head was got round. Up to this time we had been steaming out to sea. As we approached the shore, with the heavy surf breaking upon it in large rollers, the captain made one more effort to save his ship; he dropped his anchor just outside the surf, but as she swung to it she struck heavily, and sank. Fortunately the water did not rise above the main deck, and all the passengers were ultimately safely got on shore. The absence of any panic was very creditable to the passengers; it, however, was mainly due to the conduct of the two Ambassadors, who, during the whole time, remained quietly seated on the poop, conversing together, as if no danger impended. Around them gathered a cluster of women, who gained confidence from their behaviour.

Most of the papers connected with the Embassy were recovered, as were also those of the French; but the effect of the salt water upon Baron Gros's letter of instructions had been to obliterate all the writing except the signature of the Emperor and that of the Minister who countersigned the letter.

Upon Lord Elgin's arrival at Hong Kong on the 21st of June, we found the "Feroze" of the Royal Indian Navy prepared for the reception of the Embassy. All the men-of-war, with the exception of those required for the Canton river, had, together with the transports, proceeded to the north. Sir Hope Grant intended to occupy the island of Chusan with one regiment; but the ultimate rendezvous for the English force was Ta-lien-wan, situate in the south-east end of Prince Regent's Sword, the promontory that divides the Gulf of Petcheli from the Sea of Tartary; and for the French force Chefoo, in the Shantung peninsula, was selected as the place of assembly. The troops had not moved northward so soon as had been anticipated, partly in consequence of the severe losses the French had sustained by the wreck of several of their ships containing military stores.

For the defence of Hong Kong the General had left a provisional battalion of 850 men, who were selected from the regiments that had gone to the north, on account of their health and constitution unfitting them for a hard and long campaign : besides this battalion there was a regiment of Madras native infantry and some artillery, comprising altogether a force of about 2,500 men. At Canton there was the 87th and two native infantry regiments, with artillery, numbering in all about 3,500. A Sikh regiment occupied Chusan, while a force was provided for the protection of Shanghai. The remainder of the troops had proceeded direct to Talien-wan.

At Hong Kong Lord Elgin heard from Mr. Bruce that the ultimatum, which had been forwarded from England, had been delivered to the Chinese Government, with the intimation that an answer was to be sent to Shanghai by an early date. Lord Elgin decided, therefore, to proceed to that place with as little delay as possible, and we arrived at Shanghai on the 29th of June, where we met Mr. Bruce ; the Admiral and General, together with nearly all the force, had already sailed for the north.

The state of China at this time was such that it appeared there was only wanting the pressure which the weakness of the Emperor and the obstinacy of the war party were forcing the Allies to exert, to bring the whole fabric of the Imperial Government in ruins to the ground. This Lord Elgin most anxiously desired to avoid; for, feeble as the Government was, there was nothing between it and hopeless confusion. No party was in a position to acquire even the power and influence exercised by the Imperial Government. Anarchy of the worst description would have been the immediate result of the overthrow of the existing dynasty. For, as far as we could learn, none of the movements that were agitating the empire were in any way united with each other, or the result of a patriotic love of country desirous to correct abuses grown up under the Imperial rule. They appeared, in all cases where the origin of the first movement could be traced, to be the offspring of ambition, or desire of revenge for some real or fancied wrong; all, no doubt, engendered and encouraged by the knowledge that the authorities were alike helpless to protect the well-disposed as they were to punish those who defied their authority, and any man with energy, who could command a small following, soon found thousands ready to join his standard when plunder was considered the first and principal end in view.

At Canton, however, which had hitherto always been considered the hot-bed of disturbance, the feeling appeared to be better than had existed for years: the desire for trade was increasing, and the business transacted had considerably improved. But the Imperial rule was so weak that Lau-Tsung-Kwang, Governor-General of the Two Kiang, requested Mr. Parkes, who was at the time of our arrival still British Commissioner at Canton, to urge upon Lord Elgin not to withdraw our troops from that city, as he expressed himself powerless to preserve order without the moral support of their presence.

At Shanghai we learnt that the rebels had advanced from Hanchow on Soochow, and that the Imperial troops at the latter place, after offering a slight resistance, joined the rebels in sacking the city and murdering the inhabitants.

The city and settlement of Shanghai were much alarmed at the near approach of the rebels; barricades were erected across the principal roads leading into the country, and volunteer companies formed to assist the regular forces; the city itself was garrisoned by the Allied troops. The town had a very melancholy and deserted appearance: most of the shops were closed, and many of the inhabitants had fled. The Chinese authorities expected daily that the rebels would attack the city.

The French had placed a strong force in the suburb of Tongkadoo to protect the Roman Catholic Cathedral. Large numbers of converted Chinese therefore flocked to it for protection, depositing articles of value within its walls. This wealth had a strong attraction for the Fuhkien men, whose junks lay within a few hundred yards of the building; and there was much danger of disturbances arising distinct from those created by the rebels, the temptation to plunder being great, and nothing easier than in the existing state of disorder for the starving and evil-disposed to raise a cry of "Rebels!" and then take advantage of the confusion that would ensue. Such alarms, created by what the Chinese call "lie rebels," were often the cause of as great suffering and loss of life and property as if the attack had been actually commenced by the Taipings; the destruction of human life and property being the characteristics in both instances. From such false alarms and dangers it was obviously the interest of the Allies to protect Shanghai, as it was impossible to separate the safety of the European settlement from the safety and maintenance of order in the city.

The Loodianah Regiment, which had been advanced some distance into the country, was soon withdrawn, and merely occupied the approaches by which an army could advance upon Shanghai; but hitherto the rebels had seldom captured cities by means of an open advance of this nature. They generally gained possession of fortified cities by stratagem. A few men enter a town to trade and establish business relations with the townspeople; they are followed by others, who take up their residence close to one of the gates. The same course is pursued in the suburb immediately adjoining the gate on the other side. Upon the day fixed for the attempt, those inside the city, on some pretence, create a disturbance, and during the confusion which ensues seize on one or more of the gates, and hold possession of it until joined by the main body of the rebels, who, in parties of ten to twenty, have assembled in the neighbourhood. A scene of murder and plunder ensues; the Tartars are exterminated, but it does not stop there; many Chinese—men, women, and children—meet the same fate, and the lately thriving city is soon a heap of blackened ruins covering the bodies of those lately slain and violated; the country round is laid waste, the peasantry are frequently beheaded merely to strike terror to the hearts of those who might otherwise entertain thoughts of opposing the exactions of the rebels. The Imperial soldiers, ill paid, ill cared for, and worse disciplined, offer but an ineffectual resistance, as they see the chief authorities of the city and their own officers the first to fly and provide for the safety of their lives and property.

At other places besides Soochow the soldiers raised in the provinces made common cause with the rebels in plundering the country.

With the view of encouraging the inhabitants to remain, and to warn the rebels of the danger of any attempt they might make to capture Shanghai, the English and French authorities notified by proclamation that the Allies would defend the city and protect the lives and property of the inhabitants in the town and in the immediate vicinity. Notwithstanding, however, the reliance that was felt in the power of the Allies to fulfil this promise, it had not altogether the desired effect, and people continued to leave the city in large numbers.

The chronic state of disturbance and war that had for so long existed at Canton had been unknown in Shanghai, and the people were unable to act as a Canton merchant would under like difficulties. At Canton, so accustomed are they to an uncertain state of things that both merchants and small traders are able to take advantage of short periods of quiet, without embarking in mercantile transactions to such an extent as to remove their capital for any length of time from their control.

Ho, who was Governor-General of the Two Kiang, had, previous to our arrival in China, made proposals to Mr. Bruce and M. de Bourboulon, that if they would afford him aid in driving back the rebels, he would in exchange mediate with the Court of Pekin for a satisfactory adjustment of their claims. On our arrival at Shanghai we found that in consequence of the failure on his part to soothe the "Barbarians" into a compliance with these terms, and having abandoned the whole line of the Grand Canal to the Taipings, he had been degraded and was at that time a prisoner, waiting to be sent to Pekin.

It is probable that up to this time the full extent of the disturbances in the centre of China had been concealed from the Emperor; but after Ho's failure to induce the Allies to assist him in staying the rebellion, and being wholly incompetent from weakness and cowardice to do so himself, the position of affairs became so serious that they could no longer be withheld; and Ho's successor, Tsang-Kwoh-Fan, was now on his way to Shanghai to assume the government of the provinces of the Two Kiang. With Tsang, Li was to a certain extent associated. He had been formerly Tautai at Shanghai, and was now Provincial Governor of Kiang-Su, which rank gave him the right of communicating direct with the Emperor. Of this he attempted to take advantage by hinting he had instructions to renew the same kind of indirect offer advanced by Ho, and that if the Foreign Ministers would assist the Imperial Government by driving the rebels back from Soochow, and the province of Kiang-Su, the obstructing causes to the British and French Ministers being received at Pekin would be removed.

So ignorant was the Imperial Government of the power of European nations, that it thought effectual resistance could be offered to the advance of the Allied armies in the North, while, even with the sympathies of the wealthier classes and the majority of the population in its favour, the Government had been unable to suppress the disorders which threatened, if not speedily checked, to sever from the Emperor's rule the richest provinces of the Empire.

General Ignatieff, the Russian Minister, who had been resident for several months in Pekin, had come to Shanghai a few days before our arrival. A Russian Mission had been for many years established at Pekin; its members had, however, to conform to the

Chinese dress, partly for safety and partly to avoid the annoyance of idle curiosity to which they would have been exposed had they retained the European costume.

The rumours of the intended advance of the Allied armies rendered it advisable for General Ignatieff to withdraw, as, in the event of the defeat of the Chinese army, there was the danger to be apprehended that the people, in their desire for revenge, might not regard the nationality of any European within their power. He wished also to show to the Chinese Government that the moral support of Russia was given to the course of action which had been forced on the Allies by the Emperor's disregard of treaty obligations.

The General gave a very interesting account of the state of political feeling in Pekin. In the minds of the upper classes, England was associated with the quarrels from which had emanated all the disturbances which had for many years harassed the empire; they dated the troubles from which they had since never been free to the war of 1842, and to the feeling engendered by the indemnity which had been then imposed.

It was not unnatural, therefore, that we were regarded both with dislike and fear. This feeling was further encouraged by the official mandarins, who apparently considered, if we were admitted to the capital on the footing of equality we demanded, their exclusive privileges and influence would be endangered.

By the population we were little known, but that little was in our favour. Pekin and the northern districts depend principally on the central and southern provinces for grain, and since the partial interruption of the trade by the Grand Canal, the greatest portion is conveyed in large junks from Shanghai round by sea up the Peiho to Tien-tsin; the whole of this trade we might at any moment have stopped, and the distress and suffering this would have occasioned would have been most severely felt by the poorer classes. Lord Elgin was desirous to confine as exclusively as possible to the Emperor and governing body any suffering to be entailed by the coercive measures it might ultimately become necessary to adopt; and by laying no embargo on the grain fleet, he abstained from the exercise of a power and right he no doubt possessed. The result of this humane and wise policy was the feeling of gratitude which General Ignatieff told us existed amongst the middle and lower classes of Pekin, and was the cause of our finding, when the Allies subsequently landed in the north, a friendly instead of a hostile population.

When Admiral Hope returned from the Peiho the previous year, after the repulse of the squadron at the Taku forts, Mr. Ward, then American Minister, thought he would gain by diplomacy what Mr. Bruce had failed to obtain by force. He therefore opened communication with the Governor-General of Chih-li, and being still anxious to proceed to Pekin, there to exchange the ratification of the American treaty, he accepted the conditions imposed by the Imperial Government, and after meeting the Imperial Commissioners at Peh-tang, was escorted to the Capital. On his arrival there he was lodged in a small temple, but was confined to the precincts of the court-yards which surrounded it. After several days' delay, he was informed the Emperor desired the exchange of the ratification should take place at Peh-tang, the town where he had landed; therefore Mr. Ward had to return and receive from the Governor-General of the province the Emperor's ratification of the treaty.

The treatment to which Mr. Ward was subjected showed the evident intention of the Emperor not to admit any of the Treaty Powers on a footing of equality with the Empire of China, unless compelled by force to do so. Once in the hands of the Chinese authorities, Mr. Ward was powerless to act otherwise than he did; but it was to be regretted that to the advisers of the Emperor had been afforded the opportunity of displaying their arrogant presumption in the person of the Representative of the United States.

As no satisfactory reply was received to the demands which had been forwarded to the Imperial Government, Lord Elgin resolved that any further attempt at negotiation except at Pekin, or in the immediate neighbourhood of that city, was altogether useless, and therefore on the 5th of July sailed for Ta-lien-wan, where we arrived on the 9th.

The approach to the Bay is rather striking

from the high and rugged outline of the hills by which it is enclosed; in the valleys and sheltered places there are a few dwarfed trees, stunted in their growth by the cold bleak winds that must sweep over the country in winter. Two or three islands near the entrance of the Bay, which is about ten miles deep by twelve wide, afford considerable shelter for ships to anchor; there are numerous villages on the hill-sides, and the people cultivate the ground with much care, their fields almost resembling gardens in neatness. They grow wheat, maize, millet, and a grain not unlike the Indian gram; their vegetables consist of beans, sweet potatoes, cabbage, broccoli, onions, and scarlet runners, and the fruits are pears and apples, and very small peaches, &c.

The cottages, well built of stone, are far more comfortable, better furnished, and cleaner than those of the same class in the south of China.

The first division of the army was encamped on the west side of the Bay, and there Sir Hope Grant remained, with his head-quarters on board his steamer the "Grenada," so that he might cross at any time to the eastern side of the Bay, where the second division of infantry was landed under the command of Sir Robert Napier; the cavalry and artillery were also encamped on that side.

The fleet and transports were divided into two divisions: Admiral Hope remaining on the west side with Sir Hope Grant, while Admiral Jones commanded the division on the eastern shore.

Nothing could exceed the excellent condition of the whole force; it was most completely and efficiently equipped, and never were the requirements of an army more thoroughly cared for than they were by the General and the excellent Staff he had under his command.

The inhabitants of the peninsula of Leao-tie-Shan, on the east side of which Ta-lien-wan is situated, are supposed to be colonists from Shan-tung, from which province it is believed they emigrated about two hundred years ago. They appeared utterly indifferent to the cause that brought so formidable a force into their country, and expressed no curiosity as to our future plans or intentions.

General de Montauban came over from Chefoo on the 13th of July, and accompanied Lord Elgin and Sir Hope Grant, with their respective Staffs, on board the "Coromandel," to the east side of the Bay, to inspect the cavalry and artillery.

Upon our arrival at Odin Bay, which was the name that had been given the place where the troops were assembled on the east shore, we found the cavalry and artillery drawn up on the beach; the troops consisted of the King's Dragoon Guards, Probyn's and Fane's irregular cavalry regiments, with a couple of batteries of artillery, the whole under the command of Brigadier Crofton. Horses having been provided, we mounted, and Lord Elgin and General Montauban were received with a general salute. The condition of the cavalry and artillery horses was excellent. It was difficult to imagine we were in Tartary, fifteen thousand miles from England; it was more like a field-day on Woolwich Common or at Aldershot. This was the first occasion on which Armstrong guns had been employed, and they were tried at different ranges for General Montauban's benefit, after which Probyn showed his regiment to the French officers, who had never seen our Indian irregular Cavalry; they were much struck with their general appearance and their skill, both with the sword and lance. Probyn practised them at a game which is very popular with the men: A tent peg is driven firmly into the ground, and the object is to strike it with the lance whilst at full speed, and to carry it away on the point; great skill and horsemanship are required for the performance of this feat, and the French were very favourably impressed with the soldierlike appearance of the Sikh Cavalry.

On the 16th of July Lord Elgin crossed to Chefoo, to concert with Baron Gros the future joint diplomatic and military action of the Allies.

Chefoo is about sixty miles from Ta-lien-wan, on the south side of the Gulf of Pecheli. It is the first harbour of importance along the coast north of the Yang-tse-Kiang, and lies in the department of Tang-Chow, a town about thirty miles distant, which was opened for trade by the Treaty of Tien-tsin, and which possesses only a small and dangerous harbour of its own.

The harbour of Chefoo is surrounded by high mountains which enclose a rich plain covered with thriving villages. The appearance of the people is in striking contrast to those we had been in the habit of seeing at Shanghai and in the south of China. The men are above the average height, and powerfully built in proportion. In their manner there is none of the cunning, cringing, and at the same time insolent, appearance which is characteristic of the people about Canton.

The harbour of Chefoo is commodious, and good roads cross the mountains connecting it with the country beyond. We walked to the top of one of the highest hills, and from the summit had a wide and extensive view over the plains which extended as far as we could see. From the numerous small towns and villages, the population must be considerable; and from each village being surrounded by clumps of trees, a general wooded appearance is given to the country.

From the abundance of the crops, the soil must be good; the produce is the same, only more abundant, as at Ta-lien-wan. The vines grow in the open air, notwithstanding the severity of the winter. Supplies of all kinds were furnished to the French camp.'

The French named the 25th of July as the date when they would be ready to advance; they had had great difficulties to surmount, in consequence of the non-arrival of their material, the general incompleteness of their military train, and the scarcity of draught animals for their artillery; and they had no Hong-Kong or India as their base of operations, from whence they could draw their supplies.

The English army had been ready since the middle of June, thus several weeks of fine weather had been already lost, and we felt as the month of August approached, our chances of finishing the campaign the same year were rapidly diminishing. From information derived from the Chinese, it appeared that a good deal of rain generally fell in the beginning of August, and we knew that it was impossible to move across the great mud flats that surrounded Peh-tang and the Peiho forts, unless they had been baked hard for some days by the heat of the sun.

Great things were expected by the French naval officers from some small iron gunboats which had been originally built for service on the Italian lakes. They were formed in compartments, and sent out in several pieces; when put together they were long narrow ugly-looking things, deep at the stern, and drawing about four feet and a half water. They have a rudder at either end, so that in a narrow river there is no necessity for their turning; one heavy gun mounted forward. Two only of these gunboats had as yet arrived, and the French were working hard to put them together; they were merely riveted without having either ribs or cross-beams, one shot striking, would be quite sufficient to sink them, but as they are intended to fire at long ranges the chance of their being hit is small.

After Lord Elgin had met Baron Gros and General Montauban, I was directed to return to Ta-lien-wan in the "Roebuck," to communicate with Admiral Hope and Sir Hope Grant, and to request them to join Lord Elgin at once at Chefoo, so that the final plan of campaign might be decided.

On the 19th the Admiral and General arrived, and a Council, composed of the

Ambassadors and naval and military allied Commanders-in-Chief, was held on board Lord Elgin's Embassy ship, the "Feroze."

The original plan of operation had been that the English should land at Peh-tang, which is a town at the entrance of a river of the same name about eight miles to the north of the Peiho, while the French were to land on the coast some twelve miles to the south of that river, a simultaneous advance, as soon as the landings were effected, to be made by both armies on the Taku forts. The French, however, after a careful reconnaissance of the coast, decided it was impossible to effect a landing to the south, as there were no harbours, and the water was so shallow for several miles seaward that great difficulty would attend the landing of the artillery and material, and no communication could be maintained between the fleet and their land force, an essential consideration in a country so little known, and which from its appearance as seen from the shore afforded but small prospect of supplies being obtainable. Moreover, the absence of cavalry rendered their advance into the country highly dangerous, if not impossible, from the hordes of Tartar cavalry by which they might be surrounded.

After a long and anxious consultation the Ambassadors and the allied Commanders-in-Chief decided that the Allied forces should sail and rendezvous near to Sha-la-tung shoal, but out of sight of land, and some twenty miles from Peh-tang, the place of rendezvous to be marked by men-of-war sent forward for that purpose, the landing to commence on the 31st July.

After this conference Lord Elgin returned to Ta-lien-wan, and on the 23rd the embarkation of the horses began; it was exceedingly well arranged, quietly and in good order, without confusion. The embarkation of all the troops was completed by the evening of the following day, without a single accident having occurred. The embarkation of the horses was under the superintendence of Lord John Hay and Colonel Walker.

The Chusan steamer arrived on the 23rd from Japan, where she had been to obtain mules; my brother was on board of her, and he now joined our Embassy ship.

As an evidence of the good discipline as

well as conduct of the troops while on shore, the only compensation the villagers asked for injury done to any of their property was the payment of one hundred and eighty dollars—equal to about thirty-seven pounds —for the destruction of some young growing crops, in the midst of which Sir John Mitchell's division had been obliged to encamp. Such a statement speaks volumes for the good behaviour of the men, and of the admirable manner in which they were commanded; and the Chinese were as much astonished as pleased at all their demands being paid in full.

The Embassy since its arrival in China had been joined by Mr. Wade, Chinese Secretary; and Mr., now Sir Harry, Parkes, then British Commissioner at Canton.

CHAPTER III.

LANDING AT PEH-TANG.

SOON after daylight on the 26th, there was a stir amongst the fleet of men-of-war and transports, the long-wished-for hour had arrived, the fleet was under sail for the Peiho. It was an interesting sight seeing the ships getting under weigh, every available steamer being employed in towing the large sailing transports clear of the harbour, while others, impatient to be off, relied on their own efforts to beat out clear of the Islands which closed the entrance of the Bay. The steamers were dashing backwards and forwards, while the despatch vessels and gunboats were enforcing orders and bringing up the lazy and slow, and by noon upwards of two hundred ships and steamers were bowling along before a strong easterly breeze. The fleet had not the same regularity of formation as that which had distinguished the crossing from Baldjik to the Crimea, the irregularity, however, in the order of sailing made this the more beautiful sight of the two. In the Black Sea the jets of smoke, reminding one of Manchester or Sheffield, somewhat destroyed the effect; here little could be seen but clouds of canvas, and showers of spray dashed up by the ships' bows, sparkling in the sunshine.

During the night we headed the transports, and reached the rendezvous on the morning of the 27th. The Admiral had already arrived with several men-of-war, the anchorage was within fifteen miles of Peh-tang, which was nearer than originally intended. During the day transports kept constantly arriving, taking up their position in line according to the division, brigade, or regiment, of the troops on board; the Admiral having furnished each captain with a plan shewing the place in which he was to anchor, all confusion was avoided.

On the 28th the French fleet reached the rendezvous, and by the 30th, the whole force having arrived, the combined fleets were moved seven miles nearer inshore, this was as near to Peh-tang as the large vessels could approach; the bar could only be crossed by the despatch vessels and gunboats.

The weather being too rough to allow of the disembarkation of the horses on the 31st, the landing was postponed until the following morning, the 1st of August. Early on that day the gunboats and small steamers attached to the fleet, crowded with troops, and towing boats containing others, steamed slowly towards Peh-tang. After crossing the bar, and on our approaching nearer the town we found that the entrance to the river was guarded by a strong fort, and powerful earthwork on the south side of the river, supported by another on the north, their guns commanding the entrance which is narrow; the southern fort is built upon the large mud flat which extends for miles along the shore. The place selected for the landing was about 2,000 yards south of the fort. A few Chinese soldiers showed themselves, but they appeared to have no intention of offering any resistance. A raised causeway could be seen from the gunboats, about a mile and a half inland, rising apparently out of the sea of mud that surrounds it. This seemed to be the only line of communication between Peh-tang and the Taku forts, and once gained Peh-tang would be cut off. The whole of the country for miles round the town appeared to be a plain of mud. Deep ditches were cut in places, apparently for the purpose of drainage; these, from the treacherous nature of the soil, after any rain were impassable.

The 2nd Brigade of the 1st Division, under Brigadier Sutton, supported by a French Brigade, both under the personal command of Sir Hope Grant, were disembarked, a party of about 250 men forming the advance-guard. The boats being unable to get close to the bank, we had to jump into the mud and water, which reached above our knees; but the Commander-in-Chief having shown the example, we took off our shoes and stockings, and splashed and waded for upwards of half-a-mile through a mixed compound of mud and filth, until we gained the hard-baked mud. The only enemy in sight was a small cavalry picket, at a drawbridge across the causeway, about a hundred yards distant from the southern gate of the town. They appeared to be leisurely watching our movements. Before we got to the causeway we found a large intervening flat of soft mud surrounded by a deep ditch into which the tide flowed, and it was some time before we floundered through this worse than morass. When we had approached within easy rifle shot, the cavalry picket mounted and rode slowly along the road leading to Taku.

The French, who were on the left, having found harder ground, reached the causeway first, and moved at once towards Peh-tang, but were halted as soon as they came opposite our advance guard.

It was now 6 p.m., and as the disembarkation of troops was still going on, the General decided to bivouac on the ground where we then were for the night. The causeway was occupied and the communication with the landing place kept open by a couple of regiments left on the mud flats for that purpose.

The drawbridge near the town, at which the Chinese cavalry picket had been stationed, was about a mile and a half from where we were halted, and as no further advance was intended, Colonels Foley and Dupin, Captains McGuinness and Dew, and myself, walked forward to see if the bridge had been rendered impassable. We were glad to find both it and the guard-house perfectly uninjured. Crossing the bridge, and passing close to the townspeople, who were collected in groups outside their doors anxiously watching our movements, we approached the fort on which their flags were still flying, but not a soldier was to be seen. As it was of consequence, in the event of any troops remaining in the Fort, to secure the bridge, we returned to acquaint the General of the absence of any opposition, and he ordered the post to be at once occupied by a combined party of English and French. During the night Mr. Parkes, and Captain Williams of the Quarter-Master General's Department, entered the town; the former got into communication with one of the townspeople, and learned that the forts were deserted, but that various infernal machines had been so placed as to explode amongst our troops on their entering the place. Mr. Parkes insisted, as the man had admitted he knew where they were, on his immediately accompanying him to the forts to point out where they were concealed. After some little difficulty, Mr. Parkes, with that determined energy which has carried him and others through so many dangers and trying scenes, succeeded in making this man go with them, and upon the information he thus obtained, the dangers were removed by a party sent forward for that purpose. The army passed the night, not very pleasantly, on the mud-flats and causeway, without water, or anything to eat; wet through, and lying on very moist ground.

At 4.30 a.m., the gun-boats pushed into the river, and we advanced on the land side, as had been previously arranged, and occupied the town at 5.30 a.m.

The north fort being likewise evacuated, we had now complete possession of the entrance to the river, and the Admiral commenced at once to land men, horses, guns, and stores: to expedite the landing, piers and jetties were constructed, and soon the river face of the town almost rivalled in activity the docks of Liverpool.

As there was no place on the outside where the troops could encamp, it was decided to divide the town between the Allied armies.

A large number of Chinese coolies, who had been trained and organised as a military train by English officers were lent to the French, who were very inadequately provided with means of transport.

The result of the concentration of so many troops in the comparatively limited space enclosed within the walls of Peh-tang, necessitated the ejectment of many of the inhabitants from their houses; this was done as kindly as possible, yet with all the consideration that under the circumstances could be shewn to the unfortunate inmates, an immense amount of suffering was the result.

For the purpose of constructing the quays and wharfs, whole streets had to be pulled down; the people had nowhere to go, no money and no food; old women who for years had never been outside their doors, suddenly found themselves without a roof to cover them, and wandered tottering along in helpless misery. Whenever feasible, notice was given for the people to remove their goods and obtain some other shelter, but even when this was done, the poor people were seldom able to take advantage of the time allowed; for many, either from age or poverty, or from having no other place to which they could go, were unable to leave the town, while others preferred to destroy themselves and families sooner than expose their wives and daughters to the risk and danger of flight.

This was the sad fate of the family of the unfortunate man who, by the information he gave respecting the infernal machines, had in all probability been the means of saving the lives of many of the men. The second day after the occupation of the town, Mr. Parkes, surprised at his not having been to see him as he had promised, went to his house to ascertain the cause. On entering we found the lower room full of broken furniture; upstairs were five dead bodies, one man and four women, two of them young girls. The body, however, was not that of the man of whom we were in search. At last, after much inquiry, we learnt that he was in a neighbouring house. We there found him, apparently dying. From his account it appeared, a party of French soldiers came to his house and used great violence. As soon as they left, he and his whole family took poison; the French returned before he was quite dead, and removed him to one of their hospitals, and we heard afterwards that he had recovered.

When we entered the town, on the morning of the 2nd, nearly all the shops were closed, but one old man had kept his open, and welcomed a few of us who entered early in the morning, and gave us tea, a luxury impossible to describe, after being nearly twenty-four hours without anything to drink. He too fell a victim, like many others, his kindness and confidence in our protection having proved of no avail.

When we entered Peh-tang it contained a population, it was said, of some 20,000 inhabitants; what became of the large majority of that population we could never ascertain.

The people whom the Chinese most dreaded were their own countrymen, the Canton coolies, who performed the duty of military train; these had no feeling of pity or sympathy for the unfortunate inhabitants, but took every opportunity to plunder and commit other atrocities. Severe examples were made of all who were discovered.

CHAPTER IV.

STEPS TAKEN TO OBTAIN INFORMATION OF ENEMY'S POSITION.

By the evening of the 2nd, a considerable force having been landed, Sir Hope Grant decided on sending out a strong reconnoitring party along the causeway, and at 3.30 on the morning of the 3rd, a force moved out of the town, consisting of 1000 French leading, with two light mountain guns, supported by 1000 English, consisting of the 60th Rifles, 2nd Queen's and 15th Punjaub's. The causeway, from the previous day's rain, was deep and much cut up; the mud flats on either side were almost under water. After proceeding about two miles and a half, we came to a few ruined buildings, from which a picket of the enemy's cavalry retired as we advanced; about a mile beyond this the causeway ended, opening on to a large plain, covered partially with grass. About half a mile in advance of where the causeway joined the plain, there was a small cluster of buildings which the Chinese occupied in some force, and behind which the cavalry we had first seen retired. As the Allied force approached, the Chinese opened a smart fire on the head of the column; the French brought up their mountain guns and deployed a company on to the mud on either side of the causeway, advancing in skirmishing order. During the halt a few men were hit, but as soon as the above dispositions had been made, and a few rounds fired by the mountain guns, the column again moved forward, and as it reached the dry ground beyond the causeway, the French deployed to the right and the English to the left of the road. The whole force throwing out skirmishers then advanced, the English in echellon, the 2nd Queen's leading. The Chinese maintained a pretty good jingal and matchlock fire. After moving forward about half a mile, the English were made to lie down about six hundred yards from a long crenated intrenchment, which extended about half a mile across our front. A large body of about 3000 Tartar cavalry took up their position with rapidity and precision of movement on the right flank of the enemy's line, but a sheet of water lay between the ground we occupied and where they were.

As the Brigadier in command, on seeing the number of the Chinese and the strength of their position, had sent back for instructions, the apparent hesitation on our part caused the Chinese to redouble their fire; but although the shot fell pretty thick, we lost only five or six men. In about two hours, Sir Hope Grant arrived with reinforcements, but as he did not wish to bring on a general action, we returned to Peh-tang, which we reached about 11 a.m.

The navy, with an energy and skill which I believe only British naval officers and men can bring to bear, were daily landing stores, men, and horses. The state of the tides kept them employed at all hours, both day and night, but all was done with a cheerfulness and alacrity that overcame all difficulties.

A few days of rain, which flooded the mud flats and made the causeway soft and almost impassable for guns, created a filth and stench in the town, where the mud soon became many feet deep, truly awful. The desponding, and in all expeditions there are sure to be plenty of this class, predicted all manner of misfortune to the expedition; but in the minds of all some uneasiness existed for the health of the troops, crowded together as they were in a small undrained town. However, the weather again cleared, and hope was once more in the ascendant.

The French had now in some degree organised their transport and military train, and as the requirements of their commissariat department, which was conducted on the most economical system, was not so difficult to provide for as the English, no delay was likely to be occasioned by any want of preparation on their part. Beyond a ration of biscuit, some sardines, and coffee, the French soldiers, at the time of which I speak, had mainly to depend on their own exertions for further supplies: fortunately on our first arrival the supply of pigs was large, but this resource began to run short, and it was thought not improbable that some of the half-wild dogs that roamed the streets in hundreds were in danger of soon forming part of the contents of the camp kettle.

Sir Hope Grant, after the reconnaissance of the 3rd, had decided to send a cavalry reconnoitring party to endeavour to find some road across the mud plains to the westward that would lead to the grassy country which extends round the large town of Sinho, which is in the immediate neighbourhood of the Taku forts. His object being to turn the flank of the Chinese position, which was constructed with a view of opposing and crushing any advance we might attempt to make along the causeway.

On the morning of the 9th a force consisting of 100 of the King's Dragoon Guards, with 100 of Probyn's Horse, the whole under the command of Colonel Wolseley, Assistant-Deputy Quartermaster-General, assembled, at 3 a.m., at the drawbridge leading from the town. Colonel Crealock and myself accompanied the party.

To protect the rear and flank of the cavalry from a sudden advance of the Chinese along the causeway, 100 infantry were thrown forward about two miles along the road, to hold the picket-house until the cavalry returned.

After proceeding about a mile, a favourable place offered for crossing the mud ditch at the side of the causeway, the tracks of carts encouraging us to hope that we might find a way by which the artillery could be brought across. Two miles brought the party to sound ground covered with grass, perfect for the operations of cavalry and artillery, which stretched up to the town of Sinho, and in the distance, over the low banks of the Peiho, the masts of junks passing up and down that river could be easily distinguished. There were also in the plain large water-holes, convenient for watering our horses, which had been on very short allowance ever since their landing.

We observed mandarin poles erected in front of several earthworks, which at some little distance had the appearance of crenated walls and encamped positions. These we approached with great caution, but on reaching them found they were extensive burial places, garrisoned by no more alarming enemy than a few half-starved dogs.

In this part of the country, where from the

nature of the ground, it is impossible to dig proper graves, the Chinese dispose of their dead by placing the coffin on a mound raised some ten feet above the ground, and then heap a quantity of earth on the top in a conical shape, to the height of from fifteen to twenty feet. These tombs are evidently not very lasting, for a few days' rain washes much of the earth away, and it can be only by constant care and attention they are retained in such good preservation. At the distance of a mile, they have a strong resemblance to an encampment, the mounds being about the same shape and height as the ordinary tent.

During the morning only a few Tartar horsemen had shewn themselves, but when Colonel Wolseley, satisfied with what he had seen, began to retire, a large body of cavalry suddenly made their appearance, apparently brought hastily forward from some position in the rear. They advanced with rapidity and in good order, but did not approach nearer than half a mile. The object of the reconnaissance, however, having been attained, we returned slowly to camp.

Colonel Wolseley had obtained a very

satisfactory view of the disposition of the Chinese force, and was able to give a good report as to the practicability of a division of the army advancing by this direction.

CHAPTER V.

DESCRIPTION OF THE POSITION OF THE NORTHERN AND TAKU FORTS.

BEFORE the army could advance towards Pekin, it was necessary to secure our base of operation and a safe and convenient line of communication with the fleet; this could only be attained by opening the Peiho to our gunboats and smaller transports, by the capture of the forts which commanded the entrance to the river. The attention of the Allied Commanders was therefore directed to the consideration of the various difficulties which had to be overcome before an attempt could be made to accomplish the object they had in view.

By a reference to the accompanying plan, it will be observed that the Allied armies, by landing at Peh-tang and advancing on Taku from that direction, approached the northern forts in the rear. The ground on which they were built is a kind of promontory, bounded on the eastern side by the Gulf of Pechili, and protected from the near approach of gunboats by the sandbanks and shallows that extend seaward for several miles; on the south side it is bounded by the Peiho, which at this point is about a quarter of a mile wide; on the north and north-west by a great salt flat intersected with a series of deep canals having steep muddy banks.

The largest of the forts was situated on the seaward extremity of this tongue or promontory, and was of great extent. The outer earthworks, which enclosed a considerable area, were armed with heavy guns, so placed as to sweep all the land approaches; near the centre of the enclosure, were two cavaliers, open to the rear on the land side, each mounting five or six very heavy guns, commanding the entrance of the river.

About three-quarters of a mile to the rear of this fort there was another, but smaller fort, protected on the south by the Peiho, on the east by the guns of the fort which I have already described, and on the north and west by mud and salt flats.

About two miles and a quarter to the north-west of this fort is the village of Tung-ku, the intervening plain being intersected by small canals, watercourses, and swamps.

On the western side of Tung-ku there was a long entrenched work which extended from the marshy ground on the north, to the Peiho on the south; beyond this the plain opens out to about a mile in width, and extends to the tracts of grassy country which we had observed round Sinho during the cavalry reconnaissance of the 9th, impassable for artillery until the canals and deep ditches that intersected the plain were bridged over. A raised causeway, about thirty feet wide at its base, and raised eight feet above the surrounding country, connected Sinho with the fortification at Tung-ku.

On the southern bank of the Peiho, extending from the entrance as far up the river as opposite to the town of Tung-ku, there were a succession of forts able to assist in the defence of the northern forts in the event of their being attacked.

The forts I have attempted to describe were, with the rafts and other obstructions in the river, almost impregnable from any attack that could have been directed against them from the sea, and although the same attention had not been bestowed to protect their position on the land side, still the Chinese had evidently anticipated the possibility of an attack from that quarter, and as the swampy character of the ground limited the selection of the place of attack to be from Sinho and across the plain in front of the Tung-ku line of works, the Chinese had concentrated their exertions in this direction, to the defence of one or two vulnerable points. I have endeavoured to give an idea of the strength of the position, by beginning with the fort nearest the entrance of the Peiho, and furthest, consequently, from the point of attack decided upon by the Allies.

At Sinho and in its immediate neighbourhood the greater part of the Chinese army was assembled, the cavalry bearing a large proportion to the whole force.

The causeway leading from Peh-tang opens on to the plains about two miles and a half to the north-east of Sinho, and when, by our landing at Peh-tang, the Chinese

Position of the Northern and Taku Forts. 61

found their rear and flank threatened, they endeavoured, by erecting a succession of earthworks commanding the end of the causeway, to prevent any advance being attempted in that direction, while they relied on the soft and treacherous nature of the mud flat that surrounded Peh-tang for miles, as sufficient protection against our attempting a flank movement.

The capture of the intrenchments at the head of this causeway, and the occupation of Sinho, were therefore the first operations to be undertaken.

We had little authentic information as to the strength of the force opposed to us. We knew that the Imperial Government had used their utmost exertions to assemble an army sufficiently formidable in numbers to drive us into the sea, and from the still enormous resources of the Empire, we had every reason to believe they had succeeded in placing in the field a very considerable force, especially of cavalry. At this time a story was rife in the camp as to the manner in which the Government had succeeded in mounting some 20,000 men of this branch of the service.

At Pekin a force of 20,000 cavalry is supposed to be always kept in readiness to meet any emergency. The General in command draws the pay for the men and horses, and is answerable for the proper and efficient equipment of the force; but of late years the General found that he could borrow or hire horses for the few days when the time for the periodical parade came round, and therefore, instead of maintaining the requisite number of horses, he put the money which he received for that purpose into his own pocket. However, when we landed and it became necessary to collect every available soldier for the defence of the country, the Emperor ordered a review of the troops comprising the garrison of Pekin, which included this body of horseless cavalry. The General was in despair—he feared all would be discovered, but having recourse to his old plan, he was able to parade his men on the day appointed, all fairly mounted on their borrowed steeds. A whisper of the true state of the case had, however, reached the ears of Sang-ko-lin-sin, the Commander-in-Chief, who, thinking it too good an opportunity to be lost, of horsing his cavalry, moved them at once down by forced marches to the seacoast.

The Tartar horses are small hardy animals, very fast and capable of great endurance. The soldiers are fine powerful men, nearly all of them Mongols. They speak a language distinct from Chinese; they seldom wash, and do not object to eat raw flesh, and are in consequence not pleasant to approach too near; the Chinese even complain of their dirt. They wear conical shaped hats edged with fur; their uniform is a large loose coat gathered in by a belt at the waist, large boots reaching to the knee, drawn up over loose trousers. Their saddles are small, and they ride with their knees nearly as high as the pommel of the saddle. They are armed with swords, lances, matchlocks, and many of them have besides bows and arrows slung across their backs. The infantry are armed with matchlocks and jingals; the colour of their uniform depends on the division of the army to which they belong. The artillery is good, and fairly served; like all Easterns, the Chinese stand well to their guns, and exhibit bravery and coolness under fire.

CHAPTER VI.

CAPTURE OF SINHO.

THE day after the occupation of Peh-tang, the "Grenada," which was the steamer appropriated to Sir Hope Grant and his head-quarter staff, moved into the river, and as the General had taken up his quarters on shore, he handed her over to Lord Elgin and the Embassy, as the "Feroze," Lord Elgin's steamer, drew too much water to cross the bar.

For the purpose of keeping up the communication between Lord Elgin and Sir Hope Grant, Colonel Crealock and myself were temporarily attached to the General's staff.

To obviate as much as possible the inconvenience and uncertainty that is inherent in divided command, it had been arranged between Sir Hope Grant and General de

Capture of Sinho.

Montauban that they should take alternate days for commanding in the field.

The weather, after many changes, looking a little more favourable, Sir Hope Grant, who was exceedingly anxious to get the troops out of the crowded streets of Pehtang before any sickness was engendered by the smell and filth, made arrangements for an immediate advance.

On the 12th of August, therefore, everything being in readiness, Sir Hope Grant, as it was again his turn to command the combined operations, directed Sir Robert Napier to move his division along the causeway, keeping that road until he reached the point about a mile beyond the town, where Colonel Wolseley in his cavalry reconnaissance had discovered a way by which Sir R. Napier's division could gain the large plains of grass to the west of Sinho, and thus attack the Chinese in flank, while the main column proceeded along the causeway to attack the enemy's entrenchments in front.

At 6 a.m. Sir Robert Napier moved off; the day was glorious, and the expedition marched in high spirits.

Sir Robert's division consisted of two

brigades of Infantry. To this force was added the King's Dragoon Guards, Probyn's and Fane's Regiments of Horse, Milward's Armstrong and Sterling's six-pounder battery.

Time was allowed for the 2nd Division to get over the bad ground before the main column of French and English, commanded in person by Sir Hope Grant, moved out of Peh-tang, the English leading. We had not proceeded far along the causeway when we observed that Sir Robert Napier had gained the grassy plains, about two miles to our right, and was advancing steadily in order of battle. In front of us, at the end of the causeway, we observed about 3000 cavalry drawn up to oppose our advance, but when they became aware that Sir Robert Napier's force was turning the flank of their intrenchments, they suddenly wheeled to their left, and moving rapidly and in very good order, made a most gallant charge, with the apparent intention of cutting in between the main column of the 2nd division and its rear guard. The division halted to receive them, the regiments remaining in their columns of formation. Milward's and

Sterling's batteries opening on them as they approached. The enemy's cavalry, composed entirely of Mongolians, charged almost home to the guns, when our cavalry were launched at them, and after a short but spirited fight, the Chinese were in full retreat, being pursued by the King's Dragoon Guards and Sikhs.

While this was occurring on our right, the main column had gained the head of the causeway, deploying on either side as they got clear of the road, the Chinese from their first intrenched position opened a smart fire to which our batteries replied, and as soon as a few regiments had formed, Sir Hope Grant pushed forward, and when within a hundred yards of the work, the Chinese retired. We found the intrenchment unfinished, and open to the rear.

The Chinese cavalry, on being driven back by Sir Robert Napier's division, did not attempt to make a stand at the second intrenchment in front of Sinho, but retired along the road leading to Tung-ku. A bend in the line of road brought them within range of our guns, when an Armstrong and a French rifle battery made very good practice amongst them.

Sir Hope Grant, after capturing the first intrenchment, formed a junction with the left of Sir Robert Napier's division. The Chinese made no other stand, but retreated through Sinho, which we occupied.

Sinho offered a most pleasing contrast to Peh-tang; it was surrounded by well kept kitchen-gardens, full of vegetables, fresh and beautiful to our eyes after being accustomed for the last few days to look upon nothing but mud.

The town promised plentiful supplies of grain, &c., for the troops, and as immense quantities of hay had been collected for the use of the Tartar cavalry, sufficient to supply the Allied armies for at least six weeks, all anxiety on this account was therefore removed.

The army passed through the town and encamped on a plain to the south-east, about two miles from the long fortification which extended across the plain, in front of the village of Tung-ku, of which I have already made mention. A causeway, as described in my general account of the Chinese position, led from Sinho to the principal gateway opening into this intrenchment; but impassable mud ditches on either side separated the road from the plain, which was also intersected by streams and canals of such depth as to necessitate their being bridged, before any advance could properly be attempted.

As it was only a little past noon, and the troops were still fresh, General de Montauban thought that if immediate advantage was taken of the enemy's confusion, the main gateway might be forced without any great difficulty, by an attack directed along the causeway.

Sir Hope Grant, therefore, handed over the command and the direction of the movement to General de Montauban, and ordered an English brigade to support the French if required.

The breadth of the road did not admit of more than four men abreast, and as the French came within range, the Chinese opened a brisk fire on the head of the column. The French could only reply with two small mountain guns, and after an ineffectual attempt for above an hour to silence the enemy's fire, the column had to retire.

The loss of the English army during the day had been very small, not exceeding forty men in all, and I do not suppose the Chinese lost many more, for although our irregulars got well in amongst the Chinese cavalry, the speed of the Tartar horses and the difficult nature of the ground which they succeeded in reaching, prevented much execution being done; the Sikhs themselves thought they had cut down about seventy Mongols.

To prevent temptation to drunkenness, small parties under non-commissioned officers were sent through Sinho to destroy all the samshu (a spirit made from rice) with which the town abounded. They had orders also to collect grain, of which a very large supply was procured.

In the house which had been occupied by the Tartar General as his head-quarters some very interesting papers were discovered. They were copies of dispatches which he had written to inform the Imperial Government of the arrival of the Allies off the coast, as well as the instructions which he had received in reply, directing him not to oppose our landing, but to retire gradually before our armies until he had succeeded in alluring them into the open country, when they were to be overwhelmed by the Tartar cavalry.

On the afternoon of the 12th and on the following day, the Engineers had been busily employed in bridging the streams that intersected the plain between Sinho and Tung-ku.

In consequence of General de Montauban's advance after the action of Sinho, it had become Sir Hope Grant's turn again to command, and early on the morning of the 14th, everything being in readiness for the advance, the Allied armies, at 6 a.m., formed up in line of battle, the right of the English resting on the Peiho, their left on the French right. The English point of attack was the angle of the intrenchment on the river bank, that of the French the gateway at the head of the causeway.

The artillery was in advance of the line, four field and two rocket batteries in front of the English, and eighteen guns in front of the French.

As the line advanced across the plain, the Chinese opened fire on our right flank from some houses and junks on the opposite side of the river; but this was speedily silenced. When the line had arrived within half-a-mile of the intrenchment, the 60th Rifles moved forward on the right, and got under cover of some houses and trees within fifty yards of the work, behind a breastwork that our Engineers had thrown up during the night.

About a thousand yards from the intrenchment, the artillery halted and opened fire. More especial interest attached to the artillery in this campaign, as this was the first occasion on which Armstrong guns had ever been employed. The practice was very accurate and destructive; the batteries advanced three several times, and finally opened fire at under 500 yards from the intrenchment, so close that the enemy could not depress their guns sufficiently to harm them.

After an hour and a-half's firing, the Rifles made a rush for the angle at the river, and in five minutes gained the inside of the work. The Chinese stood well to their guns, but their position was too extended, and as soon as the English turned their flank, the troops who were defending the centre and right of their position gave way, and retired through the village which gives its name to the fortification. The Allies followed as far as the plain that separates Tung-ku from the northern forts. Sir Hope Grant there stopped any further pursuit.

The garrison of Tung-ku had consisted of from three to four thousand men formed in three distinct encampments. The ease and rapidity of our success had evidently not been anticipated, for nothing had been removed from their tents, their breakfasts even being only half finished. Twenty-four guns of various calibre, ranging to as large as a 32-pounder, were captured. Fourteen were of brass and exceedingly well finished.

The capture of this place opened Taku and the forts of the Peiho to the Allies. But before I proceed to describe the capture of those places it will be well to relate what had passed between Lord Elgin and the Chinese officials since the landing of the army at Peh-tang.

CHAPTER VII.

CORRESPONDENCE OF LORD ELGIN AND THE GOVERNOR-GENERAL OF CHIH-LI.

THE first step taken by the Chinese Government to attempt to ward off the blow that was threatening them, was a letter written by Hang-Fuh, Governor-General of the province of Chih-li, to Lord Elgin, dated the 7th of August, a week after the landing, asking the reason of our hostile appearance at Peh-tang, while the two nations were still at peace, and on terms of friendly relationship; if any questions did require settlement, he begged Lord Elgin would appoint some time and place for a meeting, so that they might be amicably discussed and arranged.

The letter then remarked at some length upon the proceedings of the fleet, beginning by saying it was by rumour only the Governor-General had heard of the arrival in China of a British minister, who was to proceed to the north to settle all difficulties, —that he had in consequence looked forward to his arrival, and had appointed officers at Peh-tang to wait and receive any communication that might arrive from the British minister—that none had come—but that a few days since, many vessels had suddenly made their appearance, and many thousands of British soldiers had been disembarked at Peh-tang,—that previous to that, he, the Governor-General, to avoid any chance of unpleasantness or collision arising, and also to leave the British minister more entirely a free agent, had removed the guns and men from the Peh-tang forts,—that when the fleet first arrived the Governor-General was not aware Lord Elgin was with it, but having learnt from the Americans that he was, he had been on the point of opening communications when, on the 3rd, a column (the reconnaissance on that day) advanced along the causeway with the apparent intention of taking a fortified position held by the Chinese army, but that the English were checked by the vigorous resistance offered by the Imperial troops, and had been obliged to retire. The Governor-General, however, congratulated himself that there had been no loss of life on either side, and he felt sure that the movement had been made without the consent of the British minister, Lord Elgin, but was one for which the soldiery were alone responsible. The letter wound up by requesting a meeting.

Lord Elgin had studiously avoided communication with any of the provincial officials, as he was aware they would endeavour by every means in their power to engage him in a correspondence, for the mere purpose of gaining time, for if the advance of our troops could be delayed for a few weeks, the season would then be too far advanced to admit of any attempt being made to approach Pekin that year.

Hang-Fuh therefore availed himself of a circumstance which occurred when we first occupied Peh-tang to assume that Lord Elgin had made some communication asking for an amicable settlement of existing difficulties, and his letter was written so as to convey the impression it was in reply to one that had been addressed to him by Lord Elgin with this object.

What had really happened was as follows: Water being very scarce at Peh-tang, the Admiral sent a dispatch vessel up the river for the purpose of ascertaining where any could be procured, the river water being brackish and undrinkable. After proceeding a few miles, water was discovered, but close to the landing place the officer in command observed a large Chinese encampment; he therefore landed with a flag of truce, on which were written words in Chinese to the effect, "If left alone we will leave others alone," and in a conversation which subsequently took place between Mr. Morrison, who went with the vessel as interpreter, and the mandarin in authority at the camp, the same assurance was reiterated, and the Chinese force was withdrawn a short distance to enable our men to fill the watercasks without risk of interruption. Although the mandarin was distinctly informed by the interpreter that the message was from the Admiral, the Governor-General chose to consider this proceeding evinced a desire upon Lord Elgin's part to open negotiations for the discussion of some plan that might bring about a settlement of affairs.

Admiral Hope therefore wrote to Hang-Fuh to explain that the message emanated from him, and stated his reasons for sending it.

A few days later, after consultation with Baron Gros, Lord Elgin wrote to Hang-Fuh informing him of the only terms on which he would consent to stay naval and military proceedings, which were the unqualified acceptance of the ultimatum sent to the Court of Pekin by Mr. Bruce, and the surrender of the Peiho forts into our hands.

This letter could not have been received by Hang-Fuh before another had arrived from him to Lord Elgin, written much in the same strain as the former one.

After the capture of the fortifications of Tung-ku on the 14th, letters arrived daily, sometimes two or three in the twenty-four hours, but in none of them was any mention made that the terms of the ultimatum would even be considered; the Governor-General's whole endeavour was directed to delay military operations by any excuse or means in his power, and he entertained the vain hope that he might succeed in drawing Lord

Elgin into a correspondence during which he no doubt hoped military operations would be suspended.

Lord Elgin's invariable answer was a reference to his letter in which the acceptance of the ultimatum was the only condition on which he would consent to stay hostilities.

Amongst other attempts to delay the further advance of the army, the Governor-General notified to Lord Elgin that two mandarins, Hang-ki and Wan-tsün, had been appointed to make the necessary arrangements for conducting Lord Elgin to Pekin, but as the ultimatum was not mentioned, no notice was taken of this communication.

The forts that now lay in front of the army were those that the navy had so gallantly but unsuccessfully attacked under Admiral Hope in 1859. These were two large forts on the north bank of the Peiho, and three on the south side; these latter were supported by various other batteries and earthworks.

CHAPTER VIII.

CAPTURE OF THE NORTH TAKU FORTS.

Two plans for future operations were under consideration, one was for the army to cross the Peiho at Sinho, and attack the southern forts; this proposal was strongly supported by General de Montauban and the French engineer officers; while the other plan was to direct the first attack on the northern forts.

The objections to the French scheme were that a greater extent of country would have to be traversed; it placed the Peiho between our army and Peh-tang, which was still our base of operations, from which we drew our supplies, and the position of the south forts was one of very great natural strength; they were surrounded by mud flats, and could only be gained by narrow causeways a mile and a half in length, which were protected by a cross fire from all their works, and they could only have been approached by regular siege operations, which would have occupied several weeks, possibly months, while the only advantage that could be suggested was, that if the Allies were successful, the whole of the troops which garrisoned these forts would be captured.

The arguments in favour of an attack on the northern forts, were; we were already close to them, and although the ground was difficult of approach, by bridging a few canals and streams, siege guns and mortars could be placed in battery in two or three days' time within seven hundred yards of the fort which, in Sir Robert Napier's opinion, was the key to the whole position, and from which the other forts, both on the northern and southern sides, were commanded.

For these reasons Sir Hope Grant decided on capturing the northern forts before he commenced any operations against those on the south side of the Peiho; and Sir Robert Napier was intrusted with carrying out the necessary arrangements for the transport of the guns across the difficult ground which intervened.

The principle of the construction was the same in all the forts. They were surrounded by a thick mud wall, pierced, about ten feet from the top, for artillery; jingals were mounted on the upper parapet, which was also loopholed; surrounding the walls, on the inside, were covered buildings resembling in some degree casemates, but they were not shell proof; a high cavalier rose in the centre of the fort, mounting three or four very heavy guns, the embrasures facing seaward, but the guns could be slewed round in any direction: around the outer wall were two, in some cases, three, mud ditches, from twenty to thirty feet broad, full of water, the ground between the ditches being protected by sharp-pointed bamboo stakes driven deep into the earth, and placed so close to each other as not to admit of a person standing between them. The south side of the northern forts rested on the Peiho, which flowed at the base of the wall.

The ground on which the troops could act with effect was very limited in extent, the force appointed for the service was therefore not large; it consisted of the 44th and 67th, a party of Marines, Milward's and Govan's batteries, with the heavy siege guns and mortars, and about 1000 French with six guns.

The English reserve consisted of the Buffs and a Punjaub regiment.

The great difficulty had been the bridging of the various canals, and making a road passable for the siege guns and mortars; by the evening of the 20th, however, nearly all the arrangements had been completed.

At about 5 a.m. on the morning of the 21st, as we mounted to join Sir Robert Napier, we heard the first gun fired; we galloped forward, and found the Chinese had opened on the working parties. Our batteries at once replied. The heavy guns and mortars opened at seven hundred yards, the field guns at two hundred yards nearer. The French opened fire at the same time.

A fort on the south side of the river, distant about a thousand yards, and the other northern fort, were able to offer some slight but not very effectual support to the one against which our attack was directed.

A heavy fire was maintained for four hours, Milward's and Govan's batteries being gradually advanced, the siege guns and mortars firing over the heads of the troops, who had been advanced to within about three hundred yards of the ditch of the fort, and were lying down behind some sand-banks. The Chinese fire, although constant, was not very effective.

At about 9 o'clock there was a terrific explosion; the flames shot up to a great height, followed by thick volumes of smoke, through which we saw beams of wood, stones, and earth descending; for some minutes the fort was so entirely enveloped in clouds of dust, it was thought to be utterly destroyed, but as the wind slowly dispersed the smoke, and the outline of the works gradually emerged from the darkness, the Chinese re-opened their fire with a gallantry that exhibited a determination to resist to the last.

Under cover of the smoke our skirmishers had been pushed forward to keep down the fire as much as possible, but they had hardly advanced when there was another loud explosion, but this time in the outer northern fort. During the morning eight gunboats had been attacking it at long range, and we kept occasionally dropping a shell into it from our 10-inch mortars. The storming parties were now pushed forward, and advanced cheering; they were met by a heavy matchlock and jingal fire, and one unlucky round shot plumped right in amongst, and smashed, one of the pontoons, which were being carried forward to bridge the ditches. The men had to lie down and obtain the best shelter they could find, while another pontoon was being brought to the front, the artillery renewing their fire with increased vigour. In half an hour, everything being again ready, the storming column made a rush, Colonel Mann of the Royal Engineers, and, I believe, Major Anson, aide-de-camp to Sir H. Grant, were the first across the ditches. The Chinese met the attack in the most determined manner. The English attack was directed against the centre gateway, that of the French against the river angle of the fort. There was a desperate struggle to gain the inside; for although the Allies had forced their way across the ditches at their several points of attack, the

French, notwithstanding the most gallant efforts, were half an hour before they succeeded in forcing an entrance by scaling the walls, and the English met with an equally stubborn resistance. Even when the Allies had gained the inside, the Chinese maintained a fire from the huts and buildings on the further side of the fort, to which they had retreated. This, however, was speedily silenced, and by 10.30 the capture of the fort was complete, and the Allied flags were waving from the walls. The gallant young Chaplin had placed the English flag on the centre battery, and was wounded as he reached the summit; he had been previously wounded in the assault. Amongst the guns captured in this fort we found one of our own 32-pounders, which the Chinese had taken the previous year.

As soon as the Chinese saw we were in possession, the fire from all the other forts and batteries on both sides of the river ceased, and white flags were hung out in place of the large silk war banners that had been flying up to this time from every battlement.

A mandarin, with a few attendants,

advanced from the outer northern fort, displaying a flag of truce as large as a good-sized table-cloth, which was carried 20 yards in front of him. Mr. Parkes went out to meet him, and recognised in the mandarin, a man of the name of Hwang, who had formerly been in his employ at Canton, and had afterwards been attached to the Commissariat department during the operations against that city in 1857 and '58, when his colloquial knowledge of English was of service. Subsequently he accompanied the Embassy when Lord Elgin went to Tientsin in 1858. He then received an offer of employment from the Chinese, his knowledge of English and foreigners making them, no doubt, think he would be useful in giving and obtaining information.

As Mr. Parkes found, when he spoke to him, that he was intrusted with no message, he was sent quickly back about his business, as he had evidently merely made the flag of truce an excuse, by which from observation, he might ascertain whether we were in a position to follow up the advantage already gained.

As uncertainty still existed as to whether

the Chinese, by hoisting the white flags, intended to intimate they surrendered the forts, it was necessary no time should be lost in arriving at a right understanding on this point.

Mr. Parkes, therefore, with a flag of truce, advanced across the open plain that separated the fort we had captured from the outer and larger one in which the last explosion had taken place, and which had also hung out white flags, and tried to open some communication with the officer in command, but only a mandarin of inferior rank met him, who could, or would not, give any information, simply saying that in hoisting the white flags they had only followed the example of the forts on the southern side of the river. As this discussion took place under the walls, others joined in the conversation; some said the flags had been hoisted by order of the Governor-General; others cried out, "you have only captured one fort, we have four more, you had better come and take them." As nothing further could be learnt, after warning those he saw that the officer in command of the fort would only be given until 2 o'clock to decide whether he would surrender, Mr. Parkes returned to report to Sir H. Grant, who had now been joined by Admiral Hope, the result of the interview.

The heavy guns having been brought forward, spare ammunition got up, and the men rested; at a little after 2 p.m. the General moved forward, the Buffs and Punjaubs this time leading, supported by the 44th and 67th, the field batteries being in advance. The ground was level and free from obstacles.

No resistance was offered to the advance of the force, and the skirmishers being pushed rapidly forward, the French and English entered the fort without a shot being fired, the former on the right and the latter in the centre.

In the inside there were upwards of two thousand men seated on the ground; they neither moved nor spoke as we approached. They had thrown away their arms and divested themselves of all uniform or distinctive badge that could distinguish them as being soldiers. The fort was much larger than the one captured in the morning; none of the guns had been removed or spiked;

there were a great number of them; the brass guns were beautifully finished and of various sizes, ranging from thirty-two to sixty-eight pounders.

Amongst the guns found in the fort were several that the Chinese had taken out of the gunboats which were sunk in the attack on Taku the previous year.

There could now be no doubt that Sir Hope Grant and Sir Robert Napier had judged correctly that the first fort was the key to the position. With that in the hands of the Allies, the other northern fort, open to attack both from sea and land, could no longer be defended, and from these works the southern forts could be enfiladed at short range.

The garrison of this fort having surrendered at discretion, it became necessary to ascertain the intentions of the southern forts, and the only way of doing so with certainty was to seek an interview with the Governor-General, to demand their surrender or an explanation of their conduct in hoisting the white flags which were still kept flying.

Sir Hope Grant therefore decided on

despatching a flag of truce with Mr. Parkes, Major Anson, and myself to Hang-Fuh.

At the landing-stage below the fort we found a boat rigged up Chinese fashion, but which we soon discovered to be an old English man-of-war cutter. A few soldiers pulled the boat across the Peiho, and landing us in front of the southern fort, returned to the north side. Three French officers, seeing us embark, asked to accompany us, and we of course consented.

We had anticipated that, on seeing our small party, the Chinese would have responded; and that a mandarin, with a flag of truce, would have come forward to learn our business, but as not a man was to be seen, we thought it would be best to try to get into the fort, and open some communication with the garrison. I carried the flag on the point of a lance which I had borrowed from one of Sir Hope Grant's Sikh orderlies for the purpose. Picking our way with great care and difficulty through the forest of sharp bamboo stakes that were driven into the ground between the shore and the first ditch, which, together with the other ditches, had a few planks laid across by which we could pass, we reached the foot of the wall; round the outside of this wall there was a path about two feet wide, and seeing a few men in front of us, we followed, calling to them to stop, but were unable to overtake them.

The embrasures for the guns of the fort were on a level with, and opened on to, the pathway on which we were walking, but the mantelets were closed. After proceeding some distance, we began to entertain serious fears foul play was intended; the boat in which we had come over had been taken back to the other side, and we had gone so far along the sea face of the fort that those occupied by our troops on the northern bank of the river were entirely shut out from view. Moreover, we observed, on looking through the mantelets, that the men were standing to their guns with lighted matches, within a few yards of us, ready at any moment to recommence the engagement.

After making an ineffectual attempt to induce the people inside to speak to us, we decided on turning back, to endeavour to gain an entrance by the gate on the land side. On arriving, however, at the angle of the fort where we had landed, we found our further advance stopped by a canal, but, after a little delay, with the help of the spear I carried, we succeeded in getting a few floating planks together, on which we crossed to the opposite side. The pathway we had succeeded in reaching led past the principal gate of the fort, opposite to which it turned to the westward, across the large mud flat, by a causeway two and a half miles in length, that led to the town of Taku, where the Governor-General was at the time residing.

We had scarcely proceeded twenty yards when a mandarin came hurriedly out of the fort, followed by a number of soldiers, and hastened towards us, signing as they advanced for us to go back, but to this we paid no attention; and upon the mandarin approaching sufficiently near, Mr. Parkes informed him that we were on our way to the Governor-General on an important mission, and asked the officer if he dared to stop us. The mandarin replied that he would not prevent our going to the Viceroy, but still kept in front, so that on the narrow path we could not pass except by pushing him on one side; this we wished to avoid attempting, if possible, but upon our moving forward, with the evident intention of forcing a passage, he turned and gave a signal towards the fort, on which some dozen men rushed out and hoisted up the drawbridge that defended the gate. As soon as it was raised, he made no further objection to our proceeding to Taku, but it spoke well for the opinion they must have entertained of our prowess when they considered such a precaution necessary to secure from capture by six individuals a fort containing a garrison of about four thousand men.

The rain, which had been threatening all the afternoon, now descended in torrents, so that the ground we had to walk over became, in a few minutes, a muddy swamp.

We had not gone half a mile on the road to Taku, when Hwang, the man who had brought the flag in the morning, met us. Parkes desired him to go back and tell the Governor-General that we were on our way to see him.

The road was knee deep, and we slipped and stumbled about in a manner that rendered it highly probable we should make our appearance before the Viceroy of Chih-li one mass of mud.

The people in the streets of Taku, many of whom were soldiers, although they were peaceably dressed as country or townsfolk, were collected in crowds to see us pass; they hung listlessly about rarely exchanging a word with each other, and were perfectly silent as we approached; there was, however, no incivility or apparent ill feeling in their manner towards us.

After passing through a succession of narrow, dirty streets, we at last reached the Yamun (palace or official residence) of the Governor-General, who met us at the door with great civility. I must say, our appearance was not imposing; we had had a hard day's work from five in the morning, besides the last walk of an hour and a half through a sea of mud that had extinguished any little remains of cleanliness we may have possessed; our appearance was certainly such as to justify the Chinese not only in calling but in considering us "barbarians." But, notwithstanding this, nothing could exceed the courteous way in which we were received by Hang-Fuh; to be attributed, probably, more to his fears than from any favour we found in his eyes.

The manner and appearance of the Governor-General was quiet and gentleman-like; he was about fifty-four years old, but looked much more; in height he was not above five feet four inches, he had a haggard look, with a stoop and bend of the shoulders, that belonged rather to seventy years, and his general look indicated that he did not deprive himself of the use of the interdicted drug; his eye, however, was bright, and there was much intelligence mixed with cunning in the expression of his face. His dress was a long robe of brown silk, gathered in at the waist by a silk girdle, with an elaborately worked jade clasp; from his belt he wore suspended the usual embroidered spectacle and fan holders, as also the chop sticks, and a large richly embroidered case containing a fat silver watch.

Hang-Fuh was followed to the door by several mandarins and a crowd of attendants; these, unlike their master, who had the most perfect command and control over his features, showed by their faces that the day's proceedings had been such as to cause them much apprehension. We were led through two courtyards into an inner one, in the centre of which were a few trees and flower beds. On one side opening into, and scarcely separated from this court, was a suite of rooms in which tables were prepared covered with fruit and sweetmeats ready for our entertainment. After the usual amount of ceremonious bowing and chin-chining that has always to be gone through in a Chinaman's house before any one sits down, we at last got settled in the places assigned to us.

The place of honour in China is on the left of the host—sometimes the tables are arranged close together, on other occasions they are separated, each guest having one to himself; this was the case in the present instance. Only two of the mandarins were of sufficient rank to be seated, the others remained standing round the doorways, listening and making their remarks on what was passing; they all appeared to be civilians —or if they belonged to the army they had discarded their uniforms.

We had had nothing to eat since early that morning and were excessively hungry, and much exhausted, with the tramp through so many feet of mud at the end of a hard day's work. We therefore waited anxiously for the moment when according to Chinese ideas of good breeding it would be right to set to at the food, and drink the cups of tea that were invitingly put by us.

At last Mr. Parkes signified the time had arrived, the small plates of biscuits and dried fruit were soon emptied, and all the pears and grapes disappeared with a rapidity that I fear shocked the Chinese sense of decorum. Unfortunately they gave us no solid food, and did not even replenish the dishes we had cleared. In one corner of the court-yard I saw boxes which bore a wonderful resemblance to champagne cases, out of one of which protruded the necks of one or two bottles—no doubt the spoil from one of the unfortunate gunboats captured the previous year. My bad manners nearly made me ask for one, more especially as there was a large block of ice at least three feet square, behind the Governor-General's chair, which would have iced it to perfection, but Parkes informed us it would be considered a breach of good manners; so the ice was left to perform the ignoble part for which it was destined, namely, to keep cool the Viceroy's back.

After imbibing our first cup of tea, Mr.

Parkes informed the Governor-General of the cause of our visit, that the Commander-in-Chief had sent us to demand the reason of the white flags being hoisted on all the forts, and to enquire whether it meant unconditional surrender, and if so, that he should sign an order for their being delivered over at once.

Hang-Fuh answered, "I am Governor-General, and have nothing to do with the forts." Mr. Parkes said that that was extraordinary, as the officer at the northern fort had said the white flags had been hoisted by his orders. Hang-Fuh, however, again asserted he had nothing to do with the military arrangements, but his statement that there was a Commander-in-Chief from whom we ought to ask for explanations became confused when Mr. Parkes pressed him as to where we could find him, and at last the Governor-General confessed that the General who had commanded the northern forts had been killed; that his death had thrown everything into confusion, and that he had now no idea who was commanding. He said, "Suppose I did give an order for the surrender of the forts, I, a civilian, how am I to enforce it, when the General is answerable for their being properly defended." There was some appearance of reason and truth in this statement, and Hang-Fuh offered to communicate personally as speedily as possible with the responsible officer in command (if he could be found) of the Chinese army; but as he said there was no hope of his being able to do this for some hours, we told him we could not wait, and warned him that hostilities would be at once recommenced.

Hwang, whom we had met on our way to Taku, and who had turned back to give the Governor-General notice of our approach, had been the bearer of letters from the Governor-General to Sir Hope Grant and General Montauban. These we had taken and opened, so that Mr. Parkes might guide his conduct by their contents. They were to the effect, that having shewn the prowess of our arms, and having captured the northern forts, we should be allowed temporary occupation of them, and that now no objection would be raised to our gunboats entering the river and proceeding to Tien-tsin. Mr. Parkes pointed out to Hang-Fuh the absurdity of the language, and tone of these letters, as well as the presumption it was for him to speak of sanctioning what the Allies had by force succeeded in obtaining, and that we could not consent to deliver such letters to our Commanders-in-Chief. We therefore returned them, and rose to leave.

It was however evident the Governor-General had no intention of parting with us so easily; he made a number of excuses for detaining us,—that he had sent for ponies so that we might return in a manner more in accordance with our exalted rank than that in which we had come; and when we declared it was our intention to go without waiting for the ponies, he said that perhaps the General might not be quite so far off as he had imagined, and we might possibly see him if we would only wait a short time longer. As we still persisted on starting, the servants brought us cups of tea and sweetmeats, imploring us to stop as the Governor-General wished it. So much pressing appeared rather suspicious, and made us still less inclined to remain any longer; however, at Hang-Fuh's entreaty we waited another half-an-hour, in which time it was promised the General should be forthcoming.

Although we knew to a certain extent the perilous position in which we stood, still we did not learn till afterwards the full extent of the risk we had run. It appears Sang-ko-lin-sin commanded, and it was in search of him the Governor-General had sent messengers in every direction; probably had he been found, our treatment might have been different. He had left Taku, however, shortly after the capture of the northern forts with a few followers for Tien-tsin. The half hour having expired, we insisted on going; but on reaching the street where the ponies were said to be in waiting, we found only two prepared.

Matters began to assume rather an alarming and disagreeable form, and the time had arrived when it was necessary to speak plainly and strongly. Mr. Parkes thereupon turned to the Governor-General who had accompanied us to the door, and stated to him it was our determination to walk back if they had not the courtesy to provide us with ponies; this had the desired effect, for in a few minutes more ponies were brought and we all mounted.

As we were bidding good-bye to the

Governor-General, who had now got into a highly nervous state, Mr. Parkes asked, "Have all the people left the town?" Hang-Fuh answered with some surprise, "No, why should they?" on which Mr. Parkes said very earnestly, "Then for goodness' sake urge them to turn out at once; lose not a moment; such a fire of shot and shell and rockets will open on the whole of the southern side, scarcely any one can hope to escape. We don't wish to injure the poor people, the women and children, or the old and feeble; you stand in the position of father and mother to them; it is your duty to warn them then to leave, for it is only the mandarins and soldiers we intend to exterminate."

The effect of this speech upon the unfortunate man was very great; he changed colour and fidgeted about, much alarmed and greatly perplexed; he seemed suddenly to come to a resolution, and said, "Come, dismount, and let us discuss this affair once more." We consented, and re-entered his room—he now evidently intended business; his manner changed, and his determination seemed taken, whatever the consequences might be. Seeing this, according to Mr. Parkes's instructions we became more gracious in our manner, and showed we were willing to be soothed by drinking an enormous quantity of delicious tea with which the anxious servants kept plying us, and after more cakes, sweetmeats, and pears, Mr. Parkes again stated our demands. Hang-Fuh then made his secretary draft a letter for the surrender of the forts and all fortified places on the south shore. Mr. Parkes having examined the order to see it was in proper form, the Governor-General attached his name and official seal for the unconditional surrender of all fortifications. There was a further condition attached to this order, that the position of all mines, infernal machines, &c., should be pointed out by the mandarins in command to any officers named by the allied Commanders-in-Chief.

Mr. Parkes having secured this important document in his pocket, we bade farewell to Hang-Fuh, who wished us a good journey, and insisted upon coming to the door to see our departure.

It was now late, the night dark and stormy, with a drizzling rain; we were exceedingly anxious to regain our camp as soon as possible to report the success of our mission. We therefore lost no time in starting—a number of men with lanterns had been ordered to accompany us, as well as a military mandarin, to see us safe through the Chinese lines as far as the spot at which we had disembarked, where we rather hoped, than expected, to find a boat.

We were soon mounted on our rough-coated ponies, seated on high wooden Tartar saddles, and away we went slipping and splashing through the town; the houses were all closed and the streets deserted, the noise of our passing caused the occasional careful opening of a shutter, but as soon as it was seen who the travellers were the head receded with marvellous rapidity. As we got clear of the town we met many fugitives escaping from the forts, who on our near approach tried to hide themselves in the ditches by the roadside. We moved slowly along, the dark wet mist having extinguished most of our lanterns it was with difficulty we could see the road; at last, after toiling along for above an hour, we came in sight of the high lifts of the drawbridge leading to the gate of the southern fort, from whence the mandarin had issued in the afternoon when on our way to Taku. We were seen and challenged at the same moment, and our Chinese officer rushed forward to answer it, when it was repeated, and we thought it sounded more like English than Chinese, so we holloaed out "We are English officers," moving on at the same time; we had not gone twenty yards when the challenge came again, sharply and distinctly, immediately followed by some words of command, and we heard the rattle of the rifles as they were brought to the ready; no time was to be lost, we were on the bridge and within thirty yards of the gate, we all called out together "We are English, don't fire." There was a pause, and then a voice came, "if English, advance to the gate." This we accordingly did, we found it open, and groped our way in through almost total darkness. The vast fort seemed utterly deserted; when inside we were again hailed from the walls over our heads, and were soon joined by an officer of the Buffs, who said they had taken us for Chinese and had been on the point of firing. In answer to our enquiries, he said that shortly before sunset Sir Hope Grant, seeing the Chinese evacuating the fort, had crossed over one hundred and fifty men to take possession, that they had had only daylight sufficient to see it was entirely evacuated by the garrison, but that it was full of powder, with slow matches attached to the magazines and guns, that several small explosions had taken place, and that they had been engaged going round and putting them out when our coming alarmed them; that our first answer in English had been heard, but it was thought to be a Chinese dodge to get close to the gate, and that we were very nearly being swept off the bridge by their fire.

We now discovered that our friend the Chinese officer had taken advantage of the confusion incident on our arrival to leave us without going through the ceremony of a formal leave-taking. We felt our way through the huts and along the covered batteries to the port-hole that served as the gateway leading to the jetty. With some difficulty we found the zig-zag path that led down through the bamboo spikes, the slipperiness of the ground, and the darkness of the night, making moving at all in such unpleasant vicinity to the bamboo stakes a matter of great difficulty and danger, for one false step would have been certain impalement for the unfortunate individual.

Upon reaching the landing-place, and finding no boat or any arrangements made for getting us across to the other side, we began to think we were most ungratefully used at being thus utterly forgotten. There were lights on the northern shore which made us think boats were there, but we hailed till we were tired without any good result. The wind was cold, and felt doubly so blowing through our wet clothes. Wet, cold, and hungry, for the fruit we had had at the Governor-General's but ill-supplied the want of more substantial food, and no place but the wet mud to lie down on, was not altogether a very pleasing prospect. Parkes in the meantime had reconnoitred the hold of a junk that was high and dry close to the jetty, and he decided on lying down there as it was sheltered, and said he would keep places for us, as Anson and I decided before we gave ourselves up to these lodgings to see if we could not find some better place inside the fort. After wandering about for some time we saw a light in a hut, and found it tenanted by Mr. Steward, of the Buffs, who gave us a most kind reception, and sharing with us some biscuit, asked us to remain there the night, to which arrangement, having brought Parkes from the junk, which we handed over to the French officers, we most gladly assented.

Before going to sleep, however, we all sallied forth to have a good look in our immediate neighbourhood that no matches were alight, as some of the Chinese fusees are prepared so as to burn for hours. Our precaution was rewarded with success, for within twenty or thirty yards of the hut we found a lighted fuse connected with a small magazine. This we cut and extinguished, but when I laid down to sleep I felt the chances were I might wake to find myself high in the air; however, worn out with fatigue I was soon dreaming of Governors - General, blowings - up, forts, Pekin, and home.

A hot cup of chocolate the next morning provided by our kind and hospitable host, Mr. Steward, soon drove away the cold chill with which we awoke, and we went down to the jetty to try to get across. There we found our three French companions looking most miserable after a wretched night passed in the hold of the junk; we succeeded in hailing a French man-of-war's boat coming in from the fleet, and she put us across the river.

On arriving at the north fort we found it was only garrisoned by a detachment, the General's head-quarters having gone back to Tung-ku, and, worse than all, they had taken our horses with them. There was no help for it, so, putting the best face we could on our misfortune, we started off to trudge about six miles through mud into which we sank at each step up to our knees, and arrived at Tung-ku, quite beat and exhausted, by 9.30 a.m.

Each of the southern forts was joined to the town of Taku by a causeway, on either side of which were extensive mud flats, too soft even for the passage of infantry. They therefore possessed all the advantages of strongly fortified islands. The length of the causeways varied according to the position of the fort, but none were under a mile and a half in length, while the one we passed over must have been considerably more, and except by the capture of the northern forts, this would have been the nearest distance within which guns could have been brought to bear against the works on the south side.

The causeways terminated at the forts, being connected by a drawbridge across an inner ditch, while there was an outer ditch crossed by moveable planks. The forts themselves were more carefully built on the south than on the north side, and their defensive works were stronger. They had traverses parallel to the rear wall, to protect the garrison from a fire from the sea, as well as from shells from the land approaches.

The conditions agreed to by the Governor-General were faithfully carried out, and during the 22nd and 23rd the whole of the forts and fortifications on the south side were evacuated and surrendered to the Allies.

CHAPTER IX.

ADVANCE TO TIEN-TSIN.

According to our last year's experience no obstacles existed between Taku and Tien-tsin to our advance on that city by the river, but as it was reported batteries had been erected to command several places where the sudden turns and shallow water rendered navigation difficult, it was decided to send two or three gunboats up the Peiho, to ascertain whether any serious resistance was to be apprehended. As the service was one which required great judgment and discretion, Admiral Hope took the personal command of the expedition.

It was arranged between the Allied Commanders-in-Chief that if there were any obstacles of so serious a character as to necessitate a recourse to force, the Admiral was to wait the arrival of the

General, so that the army and navy might co-operate.

The Commanders-in-Chief were fully alive to the importance of the successes gained at the Peiho forts being followed up as speedily as possible, and entirely concurred in the opinion expressed by the Ambassadors that the immediate advance of the Allied armies on Tien-tsin was desirable. To move, however, an army away from its base of operations without any accurate knowledge as to whether the capabilities of the country to be traversed were sufficient to supply so large a force with food, required a day or two to complete the requisite arrangements, and provide against all eventualities. This rendered the advance of the gunboats all the more advisable.

At 10 a.m. on the 23rd the squadron weighed anchor; it consisted of the "Coromandel," carrying the Admiral's flag, and three gunboats.

Mr. Parkes and myself were sent by Lord Elgin to accompany the expedition.

The Peiho, near the entrance, is about a quarter of a mile across, but contracts after the first eight or nine miles to about 130 yards in width. The banks on either side are generally fifteen to twenty feet high, of deep soil; there is a rise and fall of tide of several feet.

During the forenoon, it being flood tide, we got round the sharp, narrow turnings in the river without any great difficulty.

In 1858, when I accompanied the first exploring expedition which ascended the Peiho under Capt. Sir Frederick Nicolson and Capt. Sherard Osborn, the country people and villagers when we approached the neighbourhood of any village lined the banks, kneeling as we steamed past, with their heads bowed down on the ground, occasionally with one hand raised holding a fowl, vegetables, or a basket of eggs, as an offering to propitiate the unknown invaders of their country. Experience having taught them that we neither plundered their villages nor injured the inhabitants, this year there were no such symptoms of alarm on our approach, but crowds collected wherever the gunboats stopped, and provisions of all kinds were freely offered for sale.

In the afternoon the good fortune which had hitherto attended our progress left us, for at one of the turnings sharper than usual, the bow of the steamer ran right up the opposite bank. Having come up with the flood, and as the tide was still rising, it was probable that we should float off in about an hour's time; we had therefore only to be patient. To occupy the time, several of us landed to explore a village which was within a few hundred yards of where we had run aground. The villagers met us in the most friendly manner; if they entertained any apprehension, they concealed their feelings, and exhibited the utmost unconcern at our invading their country with the avowed intention of humbling their (to speak figuratively) almost worshipped Emperor. Their sole thought seemed to be to profit as much as possible by the happy chance that had sent so many "barbarians" amongst them, who paid twenty times the proper value for everything.

There are two roads from Taku to Tientsin, one on either side of the Peiho, the high embankments of which can be occasionally seen from the river.

The distance by the road is shorter than by the river, the windings of the latter being very tortuous. The country is flat, highly cultivated under a very perfect system of irrigation; there are a few trees near the villages, which relieve what otherwise would be a monotonous-looking country.

In about an hour the "Coromandel" floated, and we proceeded to join the gunboats which were anchored about four miles in advance. We learnt from Capt. M'Cleverty, who was the senior officer in command, that some officials from Tien-tsin had been on board, and had informed him that we were then within ten miles of that city; they also brought the news of Hang-Fuh's arrival there that morning—he had travelled by the road from Taku; Prince Sang-ko-lin-sin had also ridden through the town the day before on a jaded horse, accompanied by only a few followers. The deputation stated that Tien-tsin would not be defended, and expressed a hope that the lives and property of the inhabitants would be respected by the Allies.

Previous to the "Coromandel" getting on shore we had passed nine forts, all built within the last twelve months; they were placed to command the passage of the river, and also to support each other in the event of attack.

They were entirely deserted, and it did not appear they had ever been armed. In all probability most of the available artillery had been taken to the Taku forts, and one great advantage of the Admiral's rapid advance was that no time was afforded the Chinese authorities to rally their troops for any further resistance to our occupation of Tien-tsin.

The Admiral decided on anchoring where he was for the night, but at 5 a.m. the following morning we were again under weigh, and when within three miles of Tien-tsin observed the large fortifications that had been constructed to protect the town from attack either by land or by river.

Two forts, one on either side of the Peiho, guarded the river approach, their batteries commanding a long, straight, shallow reach, with only sufficient water at high tide for the passage of a gunboat. They were, therefore, admirably placed. A crenated wall with ditch extended from either fort round the town, upwards of thirteen miles in extent, heavy batteries being erected at short intervals. It was wonderful to think the whole of these works had been constructed within the last few months; if the same energy and money had been expended in the suppression of the rebellion, how much better it would have been for the Empire.

A deputation of the principal official mandarins and inhabitants of Tien-tsin was waiting the Admiral's arrival. They brought a letter for Lord Elgin from Hang-Fuh, which was of course opened. It said that all the men and guns had by his orders been withdrawn from the forts, and he therefore hoped the two nations would be at peace, and that only a few gunboats would go to Tien-tsin, for fear of alarming the people.

Before proceeding further, the Admiral took possession of the two forts; the guns had evidently been hastily dismounted, and on tracing the marks of the wheels we subsequently found some very large ones in the bottom of the ditch.

As soon as the occupation of the forts was effected, the Admiral moved on to Tien-tsin. The river was crowded with junks and boats, and the people flocked in thousands to the banks. They exhibited none of the alarm which the mandarins would fain have made us believe existed.

The squadron anchored where the Grand

Canal opens into the Peiho, and opposite to the Yamun which Lord Elgin and his suite had occupied in 1858.

No sooner had the "Coromandel" anchored than Hang-Fuh, with a number of attendant mandarins, came on board. He expressed to the Admiral his desire that we should consider ourselves as their guests, but this impertinence could not be permitted, and the Admiral gave him very clearly to understand that it was the conduct of the Imperial Government that had forced the Allies to adopt hostile measures; that we had captured the forts, and that we were now at Tien-tsin as masters; that the Chinese Government knew the terms we demanded, and that we were now advancing to enforce our just demands, and that so far from being in Tien-tsin as guests, we were there by right of conquest, and intended to hold it for ourselves. The Admiral at the same time ordered Captain M'Cleverty, with fifty marines, to land and occupy the nearest gate of the city, and requested Mr. Parkes and myself to accompany them, as from my previous residence at Tien-tsin, I knew the way. We soon reached the east gate; it was open, and, no opposition being offered, in a few minutes the Allied flags were flying from the walls. Great crowds had collected to watch our proceedings, but apparently no soldiers, none at least in uniform.

In half-an-hour our marines were comfortably housed in the guard room so recently vacated by the Chinese.

Mr. Parkes having required Hang-Fuh to provide a residence for the Embassy during Lord Elgin's stay at Tien-tsin, a mandarin was directed to point out several suitable buildings, from which we could make a selection.

Leaving Capt. M'Cleverty in command at Tien-tsin, Mr. Parkes also remaining to communicate with the local authorities, and to arrange for supplies being furnished to the army, the Admiral returned to Taku, where we arrived at 10.30 the same night. I immediately went on board the "Grenada," which had come round from the Peh-tang river. Lord Elgin and the General were on board, and it was arranged that they were to start the next morning at nine for Tien-tsin; Captain Roderick Dew of the Royal Navy undertaking to pilot the "Grenada," which, from her size, was no easy task. The cavalry and artillery were to march to Tien-tsin; the distance by road being about forty miles, they expected to do it in three days, the infantry to be conveyed by gunboats.

We had not started long the following morning, when, at one of the turns in the river, we got on shore, and had to wait for upwards of twelve hours before the "Grenada" floated. The absence of all alarm on the part of the people, and the readiness with which they brought supplies for sale, spoke well for the character the conduct of our seamen and soldiers during the last expedition had established for the Allies throughout the country.

It being dark when we floated, we had to proceed with great caution, but notwithstanding all Captain Dew's care, we were very nearly running down the small French gunboat on board of which Baron Gros was ascending the river; it was one of the small boats that had been sent out in pieces, but the plates were too thin, and the vessels too small to be of much service: they well deserved the name given them by Baron Gros— the "tin boats."

We arrived about daylight of the 27th,

without again getting on shore, and anchored below the bridge of boats.

The river in places not being so wide as the length of the "Grenada," and the night having been very dark, Captain Dew had every right to be proud of the way in which he had piloted us.

In the forenoon we landed to inspect the residence which was being prepared for Lord Elgin. The one selected was the Yamun which had been occupied by Mr. Reed and Count Poutiatine in 1858. Arrangements had been made for Baron Gros and Sir Hope Grant and their staffs in the same building.

The portion of the building appropriated to the Embassy consisted of a succession of courtyards leading one into the other, round the sides of which were various rooms and apartments, which were made available for the kitchen, storerooms, and servants. The inner court had a beautiful garden in the centre, with artificial rock-work covered with various kinds of shrubs and creepers, together with miniature hills and temples.

Opening into this garden were Lord Elgin's rooms, and those of the members of the Embassy.

On the 28th of August, it was reported that Kweiliang, one of the Secretaries of State, was on his way from Pekin to open negotiations, and to attempt to dissuade Lord Elgin from any further advance. Kweiliang had been one of the Commissioners who had signed the treaty of Tien-tsin.

On the 31st Kweiliang announced his arrival to Lord Elgin, with a request that an early day might be fixed for a meeting, as he had authority to negotiate on such terms as Lord Elgin might think it right to submit for the consideration of the Commissioners who were appointed, together with himself, to arrange the preliminaries of a lasting peace between the two countries.

In reply Lord Elgin directed Mr. Wade and Mr. Parkes to acquaint the Commissioners with the conditions on which the Allies were prepared to suspend hostilities and conclude peace. The principal terms required were :—

First—An apology for the attack on the Allied forces at the Peiho.

Second—The ratification and execution of the treaty of Tien-tsin.

Third—The payment of an indemnity to

the Allies for the expenses of naval and military preparations.

The following day the Commissioners addressed a letter to Lord Elgin agreeing to the several conditions.

The proposed convention included a provision that a portion of the Allied forces were to advance nearer to Pekin, somewhere in the neighbourhood of Tung-chow, from which city the Ambassadors, accompanied by the members of their respective Embassies, and by a large military escort, were to proceed to Pekin to present the letters of credence to the Emperor. Therefore, while the convention and the various details connected with the arrangements were being discussed, preparations for the advance of the army were not delayed.

On the 4th of September, the Commissioners raised a discussion as to the proposed strength of the escorts that were to accompany the Ambassadors to Pekin. The 7th had been the day fixed for the signature of the convention. The discussions had hitherto been conducted by Messrs. Wade and Parkes personally, with Kweiliang and Hang-ki.

Lord Elgin was so well acquainted with the character of the Chinese and the small reliance to be placed on the word of even those holding the highest offices of state, that he was not at all surprised at being informed, on the evening of the 5th, that the Commissioners had no authority to conclude any convention without first submitting it for the approval of the Imperial Cabinet at Pekin.

The only motive the Commissioners could have had in assuming powers they did not possess, was to delay our advance by holding out delusive hopes that peace would be established on the terms demanded by the Allies; fortunately Lord Elgin had seen through this deception from the first, and had been thus able to warn the General not to believe that the pretended negotiations were likely to result in any satisfactory settlement of the difficulties between the two countries.

Lord Elgin was anxious that no time should be given the Chinese to prepare new defences, bring new forces into the field, or to rally their troops from the effect which must have been produced by the severe defeats they had sustained at Sinho, Tung-ku, and the

Taku forts; he therefore requested Sir Hope Grant to adopt the measures that might be necessary for an immediate advance of the army towards Pekin.

CHAPTER X.

MARCH TOWARDS PEKIN. — NEGOTIATIONS. — TREACHERY TO FLAG OF TRUCE.—CAPTURE OF MESSRS. PARKES, DE NORMANN, LIEUT. ANDERSON, BOWLBY, PRIVATE PHIPPS OF THE K. D. G., THE SIKH ESCORT, AND MYSELF.

EVERYTHING being in readiness by Sunday morning, the 9th of September, we started with the advance guard at daylight; the first day's march was to a place called Poo-kow, about ten miles from Tien-tsin, but owing to the obstinacy of some of the mules, and the ignorance of the drivers, it was past three o'clock before we arrived on the ground. Lord Elgin and Sir Hope Grant joined us in the afternoon.

The next morning we marched to a town called Yang-tsun; passing through which, we encamped on an open plain beyond.

Heavy rain having set in during the afternoon, the drivers attached to the Embassy carts obtained permission to seek shelter with their mules in the Caravansarai inside the town; but in the morning, when it was time to commence preparations for the march, it was discovered that they had all decamped, no doubt frightened into doing so by the Chinese authorities, who would have punished their families had they disobeyed their orders.

The General decided on halting one day in consequence of the rain still continuing, and in the hope that some of the mules might be recovered.

During the 11th, parties of cavalry were sent in search of mules, but without success. Fortunately, Yang-tsun is on the banks of the upper branch of the Peiho, and as this stream is within a few miles of the road along which we had to march, the Embassy tents and stores were shipped on board some junks we seized for the purpose.

Having secured, with much difficulty, a few mules in the town, and the Commissariat having supplied others, we were ready to march on the 12th.

The start of the Embassy on this occasion was a most ludicrous one. Most of the mules had never been in harness in their lives, and the men we got to drive them were apparently as inexperienced; if it had not been for the members of the Embassy driving the carts themselves, in which they received most efficient aid from Admiral Jones, Lord John Hay, and Mr. Bowlby, who were Lord Elgin's guests at the time, we should never have succeeded in reaching Nan-Tsai, the next halting place, about ten miles distant. It was late in the afternoon when we arrived, and we found Lord Elgin established in a capital house in the centre of the town. The sun and exertion had given me a slight sunstroke, which laid me up for a time.

The following day, the 13th, we marched twelve miles to Ho-se-woo. It is a large town which, in prosperous times, contains 20,000 inhabitants, but we found that the large majority of the people had deserted their homes, and that those who remained were in great danger from their own countrymen, as gangs of robbers infested the place, breaking into, and plundering the houses. For the protection of the people, Sir Hope Grant took possession of the city, and by establishing a number of posts and patrolling the streets, was able to maintain order.

Lord Elgin occupied a house with the Embassy, close to Sir Hope Grant's camp, outside the south gate of the town.

During our march from Tien-tsin, Lord Elgin had been in almost daily receipt of letters from the Chinese authorities imploring him to stop any further advance of the army.

Three new Commissioners had been appointed by the Emperor to treat with the allied Ambassadors; they were Tsai, Prince of I, Minyin, and Hang-ki. The first was a cousin of the Emperor, and a man of great influence. Lord Elgin had, however, informed them that in consequence of the manner in which the other Commissioners had attempted to mislead the Ambassadors at Tien-tsin, he declined to sign any convention with the Imperial Commissioners until he reached Tung-chow, a city about twelve miles from Pekin.

Sir Hope Grant conceiving that it was probable the Chinese government would attempt a further resistance before they acquiesced in our demands, decided on forming a depôt at Ho-se-woo before he advanced any farther; as ten days would probably be required to obtain the stores and supplies which he thought requisite, as they had to be brought from the mouth of the Peiho, a halt for this period became necessary.

As it was impossible, during this period of inaction, to ignore entirely the Imperial Commissioners' urgent professions of good faith, and as it was better that they should think the halt at Ho-se-woo was owing to our having at last acceded to their wishes to negotiate, rather than to our being unprepared to advance, Lord Elgin decided to despatch Messrs. Wade and Parkes to Ma-tow, a small village about halfway between Tung-chow and our present halting place, to meet the Commissioners, whom he understood were there.

On the 14th they started on this mission, and returned the following morning with the most unexpected intelligence that they had been completely successful; on their arrival at Ma-tow, they found that the Commissioners had gone to Tung-chow, where Wade and Parkes immediately followed them, and after a discussion of eight hours, the terms of a convention were definitely agreed upon. It was arranged that the allied armies were to advance to within ten or twelve miles of Tung-chow, where they were to remain, while the Ambassadors proceeded, accompanied by a large escort, to Pekin. It was agreed also that Mr. Parkes was to return on Monday to Tung-chow to make a few final arrangements.

On Sunday, the 16th, we had Church service in the large temple we inhabited, the principal room of which we used for this purpose; it was the last service many of those present were ever destined to attend.

Lord Elgin had decided on sending me with Mr. Parkes; Mr. De Normann, a member of Mr. Bruce's Legation, temporarily attached to the Embassy, and Mr. Bowlby, the *Times*' correspondent, both obtained permission from Lord Elgin to accompany us; and on Monday morning, the 17th of September, at daylight, we started for Tung chow, which is about twenty-five miles distant from Ho-se-woo. We had an escort of six of the King's Dragoon Guards, and twenty sowars of Fane's Horse, the whole under the command of Lieut. Anderson

Colonel Walker, Quarter-master-general of cavalry, and Mr. Thompson of the Commissariat, also accompanied the party; the former to select the ground for the encampment of the army, as the General, in consequence of the prospect of peace, had decided to move forward on the morning of the 18th.

It was a lovely, cool morning, and we set forward in high spirits, for we thought we saw the prospect of an early and successful termination to the war. We got as far as Ma-tow without seeing a soldier; as we passed through that village, which seemed nearly deserted, we saw a picket of some thirty cavalry, a little distance off the road on our left; they slowly retired as we advanced, and were soon lost sight of behind some trees. After this we passed occasional pickets, but they took no notice of us, except by quietly falling back further from the road as we advanced.

About ten miles from Tung-chow we passed the place where it had been agreed between the Commissioners and Messrs. Wade and Parkes that the army should halt while the Ambassadors proceeded to Pekin.

It is called the Five-li-point, and is marked by a small stream running in a north-easterly direction a distance of about four miles, when it falls into the Peiho. The plain to the right of the road, and to the south of the stream, was where the Imperial Commissioners suggested the allied armies should encamp. On the south of the rivulet is a bund or bank stretching away from the road to the Peiho; on the left of the road, opposite the bund, is a small village surrounded with trees growing close together.

Beyond seeing a few trees felled near the village, we observed no indications of any preparations being made to obstruct the peaceable occupation of the ground by the allied armies.

About four miles beyond the Five-li-point, we passed through Chang-kia-wan, which is a walled city of some size; here we were met by a military mandarin, accompanied by a troop of cavalry, who said he must know our business before he could allow us to proceed.

Mr. Parkes informed him we were going to Tung-chow to meet the Imperial Commissioners; on hearing which, he immediately allowed us to pass. We had scarcely reached the middle of the town, when a party of mandarins galloped up to us; one of them, evidently a man of high rank from the deference shown to him by his companions, asked which was Mr. Parkes. On his being told, he mentioned that he was the general who had commanded at the battle of Sinho, the result of which action to himself personally we could see, he said, and pointing at the same time to the button on his hat, the colour of which is distinctive of the rank of a mandarin, we saw, instead of its being of a light red colour, that it was only a plain white button; he also said he had been deprived of the peacock's feather, which may be considered as somewhat similar to one of our orders of knighthood—but he added, "It will be peace now, and I shall be glad to take by the hand those who fought me that day." Parkes mentioned Colonel Walker as being the senior officer present, and we were then all presented. His manner was cordial and gentlemanlike, and very attractive from his manly soldierlike appearance; he rode some distance with us, talking over the events of the campaign, and then said he must return to his camp, which was at some distance.

We arrived at Tung-chow, after a ride of twenty-five miles, about 10.30 a.m. We entered the city at the south gate, and were guided through the town by men sent for that purpose, passing out at the east gate into the surburb, where a temple had been prepared for our reception. The streets were broad and good, and we were much struck at the amount of butchers' meat exhibited for sale, never having witnessed a similar display in any other town in China.

We found a message waiting our arrival from the Imperial Commissioners, saying they would be ready to confer with the officers sent by Lord Elgin, at one o'clock; this gave us time to wash and breakfast.

At a little after one the Commissioners arrived, and Mr. Parkes and I proceeded to visit them. After the usual ceremony of tea drinking and compliments, Lord Elgin's letter, accepting the conditions of the Convention that had been previously discussed between the Commissioners and Messrs. Wade and Parkes, was read. In this letter, Lord Elgin stated that he hoped no time would be lost in making suitable arrangements for the reception of the Ambassadors at Pekin, and for the delivery of the letter of credence to the Emperor, with which he was charged by Her Britannic Majesty.

The Commissioners, to our surprise, commenced by raising difficulties instead of attempting to remove any that might exist, and refused to discuss any of the terms of the Convention until the demand to deliver the letter of credence to the Emperor was abandoned. They insisted upon the impossibility of this requirement being complied with, and notwithstanding Mr. Parkes's assurance that it was a question open for future discussion, and one the refusal of which would not be considered by Lord Elgin as a *casus belli*, they refused to enter on the other matters, which, as the allied armies were to advance the following morning to the Five-li-point, were to us of more immediate importance.

The tone adopted by the Prince of I and the other Commissioners was almost offensive, and they scarcely cared to conceal the repugnance with which they viewed us, and their disinclination to come to terms. At last, at about 6 p.m., when Mr. Parkes had almost lost hope of any satisfactory termination to the discussion, a sudden change took place in the manner of the Commissioners. Parkes's reiterated statement that their objections to the personal delivery by Lord Elgin of the Queen's letter was a question to be settled by discussion, not by fighting, at last appeared to satisfy the Commissioners, and they also abandoned a feeble opposition they had been maintaining all the afternoon to Lord Elgin being accompanied to Pekin by so large an escort as a thousand men.

The Commissioners went now fairly into the business matter before them, and the necessary arrangements for the encampment of the army on the following morning, and providing them with the requisite supplies were quickly settled. A proclamation was likewise drafted to inform the people that peace had been established between the Emperor of China and the Allies.

We thought our difficulties were now drawing to a close, and after a day of much anxiety and hard work, Parkes joined us at dinner, Hang-ki coming frequently during dinner to settle various points with reference to the proclamation. We all went to bed early.

It had been arranged that Colonel Walker,

Mr. Thompson of the Commissariat, Mr. Parkes, and myself, accompanied by six Dragoon Guards and three Sikhs, should start early in the morning, and meet the allied armies, to point out the ground which had been selected for their encampment, and as Parkes and I, after communicating with the General, intended to return to obtain a residence for the Embassy, and to complete some of the minor details of the convention, Messrs. De Normann and Bowlby, and Lieutenant Anderson, with eighteen Sikhs, were to remain in Tung-chow.

At a little after daylight on the morning of the 18th of September, we were all up and breakfasted together; those who had decided on remaining in Tung-chow making their arrangements for shopping in the town.

The sun had scarcely risen when the party going to meet the army had mounted. We rode through the eastern suburb, instead of passing through the city, the way we had come the day before, and in five minutes we were in the open country. It had been arranged that one or two mandarins were to meet us at the Five-li-point. The country was flat and open, and we rode by bye-paths and roads direct for the fortified town of Chang-kia-wan, through which the road passed. As we neared the town we met parties of infantry and jingal men moving in the same direction as ourselves. The gates of the town were open, but we found considerable bodies of troops in the streets; they, however, offered us no molestation. Upon clearing the town, we had a view over the country that intervened between us and the Five-li-point, about four miles distant; the banks on either side the road rose in some places higher than a man's head on horseback. The country on the right of the road looking from Chang-kia-wan was much intersected with deep nullahs or dry watercourses; upon the other side of the road large fields of millet, which at this time of the year was from fifteen to twenty feet high, afforded sufficient shelter for the concealment of a large force. A nullah three or four miles in length extended from a little to the west of the town of Chang-kia-wan, in a semicircular form, to the village surrounded with trees, which I mentioned as being on the opposite side of the road at the Five-li-point.

Looking towards the nullah on our right as we advanced, we thought we observed some movement in that direction. I cantered across the intervening country, and found, concealed in the watercourse, upwards of a thousand cavalry dismounted, drawn up in two ranks, the men standing at their horses' heads. I rode into the nullah, and walked my horse slowly in front of the line; not a word was spoken, nor any attempt made to interfere with me. Mr. Parkes shortly joined me, and we followed the windings of the dry watercourse till we reached the village to which I have already referred; to regain the main road, we had to pass through the principal street, and there we found a large body of infantry concealed behind the houses and in the gardens adjoining. We had nearly cleared the village, when we came suddenly on a masked battery of twelve guns, in the preparation of which the Chinese were working hard. To ascertain the size of the guns, and their line of fire, we rode into the battery. This was strongly objected to by the mandarin in command, who directed us to leave the work.

Upon regaining the road on the other side of the village, we found Colonel Walker, and those with him, waiting somewhat anxiously for our return; they had just perceived a large body of infantry lying down behind the bund, which I have already described as extending from the Five-li-point for several miles towards the Peiho. The country that intervened being wooded, and the tall millet still uncut in many of the fields, rendered any distant view impossible, while it afforded excellent shelter for the concealment of large bodies of men; the plain on the south of the bund, over which our army was to advance, was comparatively open country.

The top of the embankment being wide enough for men on horseback, we rode along it for some distance, hoping to meet a mandarin of sufficient position, who could explain why the ground on which our army was to encamp was thus occupied by a Chinese force. However, to Parkes's repeated inquiries, we always received the same answer: "The General is many li away."

A large body of cavalry was now observed moving across the plain, between the embankment and the line of march of the allied armies; from the extent of ground they covered, there could not have been less than six or seven thousand. The infantry, which I have mentioned as lying down, were within a few feet of us; batteries were formed along the embankment at intervals; and numbers of troops were constantly arriving from the rear.

The position in which we found ourselves was a most critical one; it was now only too apparent that treachery was intended. Our army might arrive at any moment, possibly unprepared for the attack evidently intended to be made on our advancing columns, and although there could be no doubt as to the result, an unexpected attack of this nature might entail additional loss on the Allies.

Notwithstanding all he had seen, Parkes could scarcely persuade himself that this deeply devised breach of faith was with the knowledge of the Prince of I, the principal Commissioner. After a hasty council, it was decided that, to prevent any immediate attack being made on our party, it was desirable to abstain from exhibiting any distrust; Colonel Walker, Mr. Thompson, and five of the King's Dragoon Guards, were therefore to remain moving backwards and forwards along the embankment, ready on the first appearance of hostility to turn their horses' heads and gallop for their lives over the plain, across which the allied forces would be advancing. Parkes decided on riding back to Tung-chow to ascertain from the Prince of I himself, if possible, the true cause of the threatening appearance of affairs, and to warn those we had left behind of their danger; Private Phipps of the King's Dragoon Guards, and one Sikh, bearing a flag of truce accompanied him. I agreed to return to the road and endeavour to pass through the Chinese cavalry in front, and convey intelligence of the position of the Chinese army to the Allied Commanders-in-Chief; the two remaining Sikhs were to accompany me. Caring less apparently for concealment than they did at first, strong cavalry pickets were being thrown forward along the line of the main road. As soon as we had arranged our several duties, bidding each other good-bye, we started on our respective missions. The first Chinese line of cavalry I had to pass through was about a quarter of a mile in advance of the village have so frequently mentioned. As they made no movement to stop us, we did not check our horses, but pushed on at a canter through their open ranks. I had not ridden half a mile farther, when I came in sight of the advance-guard of our army. Observing Captain Brabazon to be with it, I pulled up for a moment, and asked if he would order them to halt until I had seen the General, who he told me was with the head of the column, about half a mile in rear; this he immediately did, and galloped back with me. When I joined Sir Hope Grant, he had just halted the army, having observed large masses of cavalry threatening his flank, and had given orders for massing the baggage in a village close in his rear, and for the regiments to form up in column as they arrived on the ground. I related to the General as briefly as possible the state of affairs, describing the general position of the enemy so far as we had been able to observe it from the bund and village; I further pointed out that the only chance of safety for Parkes and those at Tung-chow was that two hours at least should be allowed before any attack was made on the enemy's position.

L

The French army was on the right of the English, and General de Montauban now joined Sir Hope Grant. He at first urged an immediate attack; but Sir Hope Grant promised to keep off the engagement for two hours if possible, though, as he truly said, it might be forced on him at any moment.

Having now given all the information in my power, I requested permission to return to Tung-chow to rejoin Parkes and the others, to urge on them the utmost expedition, and, if possible, endeavour to find some other road by which we could extricate ourselves.

Two Sikhs, of Probyn's Horse, were ordered to accompany me, as the horses of those I had brought back were knocked up. One of the two who now went with me, and for whom I shall always entertain an affectionate recollection, was Nal-sing. I gave him a white handkerchief, which he stuck on his spear's point to act as a flag of truce, and we galloped back along the same road by which I had passed out from the Chinese position. Brabazon, who it appears had obtained General Crofton's permission to accompany me, followed at a hand gallop. It was too late then to persuade him to go back, the task I had undertaken was an almost hopeless one, and there was no use endangering more lives than were already in jeopardy. We passed the advanced Chinese line of vedettes, but were stopped on arriving at the in-lying picket. However, riding up to the Colonel in command, I pointed to the flag, bowed and chin-chined, and before he had made up his mind what to do, we were past, and going at a hard gallop straight for Chang-kia-wan. Even in the short time that had elapsed since I had passed in the morning a great change had taken place, —troops of all arms were hurrying to the front, some marching along the road, others coming across the country from all directions. On reaching Chang-kia-wan the streets were so crowded we could only move very slowly; but as soon as we were again in the open country we did not draw rein until we reached the temple in the suburbs of Tung-chow, where we had passed the night.

On our arrival we found the Sikh escort, unaware of any impending danger; and none of the gentlemen had returned from the town, where they had gone some hours before to visit the various curiosity shops. As Parkes did not speak Hindostanee he had only, we were told, on his return left a note on the table, and had ridden away through the gates of the city.

Parkes's letter was to warn the first who might come home, to get everything ready to attempt an escape, and stated that he had gone to try to find the Prince of I.

We immediately ordered the Sikhs to saddle the horses, and make every preparation for an immediate start; and I despatched a note to Parkes asking him to come back at once. In five minutes the whole party returned. Being now very anxious for Parkes's safety, De Normann and I, accompanied by two sowars, rode into the town to search for him. We had not gone above half a mile when we met him; he had seen the Prince of I, who informed him that until the question of delivering the letter of credence was settled, "there could be no peace, there must be war." Parkes quietly took down his words in writing, and then perceiving from the offensive tone assumed that no time was to be lost in making his escape, galloped out of the courtyard where he had had the audience.

On our return to the temple we found the whole party mounted and waiting. We moved off at once, and as soon as we were well clear of the streets, broke into a sharp canter. The distance we had to ride was rather above ten miles, and we had now but a short time in which to travel this distance, even if Sir Hope Grant succeeded in giving the two hours for which I had asked.

We had not gone far when Parkes's horse fell, and rolled over with him; he was fortunately unhurt, and immediately remounted. De Normann was riding a small Tartar horse, not larger than a pony, and which was neither fast nor in good condition. Bowlby's horse also soon showed evidence of distress; mine was fortunately still fresh, although he had already carried me that morning not much under thirty miles. We reached Chang-kia-wan without interruption. As we entered the town we pulled up to a walk, both to breathe the horses, and because the streets were now so crowded we could not have gone at a more rapid pace. At this time I was riding in front with Anderson, who commanded the escort; Parkes and Brabazon followed, and then came Bowlby and De Normann; Private Phipps and the Sikhs, eighteen in number, were all close up.

As soon as we cleared the town and began to descend the small declivity beyond, we galloped forward, intending to pass along the road which ran through the centre of the Chinese army. The ground on either side being so intersected, as I have already described, by dry watercourses, we considered our best chance was to push through by the shortest road before the engagement commenced.

The banks of the road, which rose occasionally to some height, were now lined with matchlock men, supported where the banks were level, or nearly so, by large bodies of cavalry. These troops extended, as far as we could see, to the Five-li-point.

We had scarcely cleared Chang-kia-wan, when the bursting of a shell in the air told us the battle had begun; the batteries on both sides immediately opened. We were at that moment in the middle of the Chinese army, our retreat was cut off, and the nature of the ground on either side prevented our attempting, except as a last resource, to force our way round the flank of the army; we therefore continued to push forward at a gallop. De Normann's and Bowlby's horses being unable to go the pace, they had fallen behind, and were in danger of being cut off by the cavalry, which were now crowding upon our flanks and rear; we therefore halted to let them rejoin us, and to decide what we should do. If we continued along the road it was evident we should be shot down without being able to raise a hand in our own defence, as at a short distance in front, where the banks were rather higher, they were lined for upwards of a mile by infantry, who were only waiting to open fire until we passed along the road below them.

Poor Brabazon at this time said, "I vote Parkes decides what is to be done," Parkes having previously remarked some one must direct and decide for us all.

After a short consultation, it was decided that we should now make an effort to get on to the plain to the right of the road, and endeavour, notwithstanding the obstacles of the ground, to charge through the enemy for a distance of from three to four miles, in the hopes of getting clear round their right flank, and then by a considerable circuit, rejoin the Allied armies. But at the moment that some of us reached the top of the bank, a mandarin, who stated that he commanded that part of the Chinese army, came forward, and said, he observed we were bearers of a flag of truce, and that therefore we were sacred from attack, unless we ourselves provoked it. He also said he would be reluctantly compelled to order the troops to fire down upon us, if we persisted in the attempt to force our way through the very centre of the Chinese position; but that he would procure a pass from the Commander-in-Chief that would enable us to go round the flank, without which order, however, he said, he could not permit us to do so; he said the General was close by, and that he would send for the pass, or, time would be saved, he said, if any two of us would accompany him to the General.

This was exceedingly plausible, and we consulted as to the best course to be pursued.

If we decided on attempting to fight our way, we at once surrendered any protection afforded by the flag of truce, and it gave De Normann and Bowlby, who were badly mounted, scarcely any hope of escape, and for the rest of us the chances were bad, as we would have to run the gauntlet of nearly the whole Chinese army for several miles, over very bad ground. The question to be considered therefore, was, what amount of reliance could be placed on the proposal.

It appeared to be made in all sincerity, and subsequent events justified this belief. It was a reasonable demand, and one we should have required under similar circumstances, and we felt that we were scarcely justified to be the first to violate the privileges accorded to a flag of truce, at all events, until we had tested the value of the offer made by the Chinese General; for if the safe conduct was refused, we should not be in a worse position than the one we then were in, and being absolved from the obligations that attached to us as bearers of a flag of truce, could then do our best to fight our way out.

In moments such as these decisions must

be arrived at quickly, and although perhaps the reasons I have stated for the manner in which we acted, scarcely found expression in speech, they were those which guided our conduct; we agreed that two of us should accompany the mandarin, and Parkes, turning round, said, "I will go, if Loch will accompany me;" at this time we had two flags of truce flying, one belonging to the escort, the other my handkerchief, which was still on Nal-sing's spear-head. I called him to come with us, and with a hasty good-bye to the others, saying, "We shall soon be back," galloped off with the Chinese officer. I shall never forget my last view of that party. The Sikhs were leaning forward on their horses to ease their breathing and to watch what was passing; Anderson, Brabazon, and De Normann were talking together in a group; while Bowlby, about a horse's length distant, looked exhausted and anxious, and was drawing his revolver from its case. He had often expressed a wish to see how the Chinese could really fight, and as I passed him I said, "I think, Bowlby, you'll soon have your wish fulfilled." We turned off the road to the left, millet still standing in many of the fields, concealing from our view any large expanse of country. We had not left our party half a mile when, on turning at a gallop the corner of one of the millet fields, we were, before we could check our horses, in the midst of a large body of infantry, who seized our bridles and pressed their matchlocks against our bodies; no time was to be lost, the Chinese officer, under whose safe conduct we were, rushed between us, and calling out in Chinese "not to fire," at the same time striking right and left. This enabled us to clear our horses' heads, and we then spurred through the troops. About fifty yards in rear was a small stream that falls into the rivulet that passes by the Five-li-point: on the banks of this small river we halted, the Chinese soldiers at the same moment raising the cry, "Sang," "Sang!" and down to the opposite bank galloped Sang-ko-lin-sin, the Commander-in-Chief of the Chinese army, surrounded by a numerous staff.

Parkes immediately addressed the Prince, pointing to our flag of truce, and requested a free pass for our party through the Chinese army. His only reply was a derisive laugh, and a torrent of abuse; he accused Parkes of being the cause of all the troubles and difficulties that had arisen; he said, not content with attempting to impose conditions which would have been derogatory to the dignity of the Emperor to accept, he had now brought the Allied armies down to attack the Imperial forces. Parkes turned to me and said: "I fear we are prisoners." We pulled back our horses, and took a look round to see if there was any way by which we might attempt to escape. By this time the Chinese infantry had formed in all round us, pressing the muzzles of their matchlocks against our bodies, waiting only for the signal to fire to be given. One glance told us how hopeless any resistance would be, and as we attempted to push forward, we were half pulled, half knocked off our horses. I told the old Sikh, who kept his eyes constantly on me, to cease to struggle further. We were scarcely on the ground when our arms were seized, and twisted behind us, and we were thus shoved forward to the bank of the stream, where a couple of flat-bottomed boats were laid lengthways across it; over these we were half carried, and shoved down on our knees before Sang-ko-lin-sin, who threatened and stormed at us, the men behind cuffing us on our heads and faces, one man seizing me by the back of the neck and rubbing my head and face in the dirt. Sang-ko-lin-sin told Parkes to stop the battle, and to send to the Allied generals to say they were at once to halt their troops; and upon Parkes laughing, and telling him his request was absurd, that, even if he had been willing, he was quite unable to give any such order, much less have it obeyed, the Prince told him he lied, and that he would teach us what it was to speak to high officers of the Celestial Empire in the manner in which they had been addressed yesterday. The Prince was evidently working himself into a fury, when, fortunately, an officer galloped up and said his presence was required in front.

As soon as Sang-ko-lin-sin left, we were hurried along about two hundred yards, towards a small cluster of houses, in the direction where we knew by the firing that the Allied armies were pressing hard on the Chinese.

A Tartar cavalry escort was drawn up in front of a small clump of trees close by, in the centre of which there was a tent pitched for the second in command of the Chinese army, whose head-quarters these were. This officer received us with civility, and allowed us to sit down; he discussed the state of affairs with Parkes, deplored the failure of negotiations, which he said the Chinese army had hoped would have brought the war to a happy conclusion. He said we were foolish to be so obstinate, and that we had far better do what Sang-ko-lin-sin required, and send the Allied armies away.

As the firing every moment appeared to approach nearer, and it became evident that the Chinese in this part of the field were not holding their own, the General seemed to consider that the time had at last arrived when it was incumbent upon him to take a more active part in the battle; he therefore rose, civilly bade us good-bye, leisurely mounted his horse, and rode away to the front.

Alarm was now evidently spreading amongst the Chinese, and they eyed us in anything but a pleasant manner. Our horses had been brought up close to where we were sitting, but were too well guarded to afford any hope of escaping on them. I was allowed, however, to take a small book out of one of my saddle-bags.

Sang-ko-lin-sin's orders being that we were to be taken to the Prince of I, a common country cart, drawn by four mules was provided for our conveyance. In it we found two French soldiers, one a young man of about nineteen, who having strayed too far from his regiment had been captured in a house which I apprehend he had entered for the purpose of looting; the other was an older man, attached to the French commissariat department. Into this cart Parkes, myself, and Nal-sing were also put. We were then driven off at a sharp trot, guarded by an escort of fifty Tartar cavalry, towards Pekin.

There being no springs to the cart, the jolting over the rough roads of the country was dreadful to bear. As the sounds of the battle became fainter and fainter, our hearts grew sick within us, and we thought much of what our poor comrades would be doing. We earnestly hoped that, finding that we did not return, they would have guessed the cause, and made an effort to escape, either round the flank of the Chinese army, or by a dash along the road. We listened attentively for any sound of firing from the direction in which we had left them, and at times we almost fancied we heard the roll of musketry in that direction.

We were first driven back to Tung-chow, and carried as prisoners through those streets which we had traversed but the day before as welcome guests escorted by mandarins of high rank; the townspeople, who then made way for us with respect and fear, now crowded round and gazed with insolence and contempt on our fallen state. We entered the eastern gate, and hearing that the Prince of I had left for Pekin, our escort immediately followed.

Poor Parkes suffered much in mind and body, and yet maintained outwardly an appearance of calm indifference to all that could be done to him by way of insult and bodily hurt.

The crowded state of the streets prevented our going very fast, but as soon as we were outside the gates the mules were urged forward at a gallop. The road leading from Tung-chow to Pekin is formed of large paving stones, two to three feet square, these not being joined very closely together, and the ruts and holes from six to twelve inches deep, make the travelling over it in a springless cart even at a walk, a matter of great discomfort, but when that pace was increased to a gallop it was the most intolerable agony I ever experienced, and seemed to threaten the dislocation of every joint.

Our escort had evidently great difficulty in ascertaining where the Prince of I had gone, for after crossing the bridge of Pah-le-Chiao, which is about three miles on the road towards Pekin, we halted; and after enquiries had been made of some troops encamped on the road side, we recrossed the bridge, and turning off the highroad, were taken towards a large encampment that was formed about half a mile distant, near a temple and some villages. Here we were taken out of the cart and hurried towards a large tent, which Parkes ascertained to be the head-quarters of Juilin, who was Commander-in-Chief of an army distinct from that of Sang-ko-lin-sin; he was likewise a Minister of State.

Juilin was seated near the door of his tent, and we were forced down on our knees before him, men keeping our arms twisted behind us, and pulling our hair and beards. He asked Parkes an immense number of questions — as to the intentions of the Ambassadors — the strength of the Allied armies, and the number of guns, cavalry, infantry, &c.; to all which Parkes gave more or less correct replies. The examination continued so long, and was so tedious, that Parkes at last whispered to me: "I must bring it to an end; I am going to pretend to faint;" and immediately fell over against me. We were then removed into a small temple close by, where for the first time we were carefully searched; all papers, as well as our watches, rings, &c. being taken from us. One ring, however, on my left hand escaped their notice, and very fortunate did I deem myself afterwards that it had not been observed.

Parkes and I were now left alone; we were in a small room, with a raised bench like a soldier's guard-room bed on one side. Being both much exhausted, for we had ridden that morning above thirty miles, and since then had been fearfully jolted in the cart, without having tasted food since daylight, we lay down together on the bench, and after speaking a few words to each other, supporting our heads on each other's legs, were soon in a sound sleep.

From this we must have been awoke in about half an hour. We were then taken through a courtyard into which a large room opened; in this room were seated several mandarins, some of whom we recognised as having been in attendance on the Prince of I, and the other Commissioners the previous day. We were again forced upon our knees. They insisted that I could speak Chinese, and that I concealed my knowledge of the language. I was kicked and had my beard pulled when I could not reply, and Parkes was beaten when he told them I did not understand their language.

In the midst of the examination we heard a disturbance in the courtyard; messengers came hurriedly in, and whispered to the mandarins something that appeared to discompose them greatly. After consulting together, they all rose and left the room; the men who had been holding us also ran away. We got up and shook ourselves, and speculated as to the probable cause of this extraordinary conduct, and presumed that some rapid advance of our cavalry had terrified them.

While we were thus standing, talking together, with a loud shout a number of soldiers rushed in, seized us, and bound our arms by the wrists tightly behind our backs. No mandarins were with the soldiers, and Parkes told me he thought from their remarks that we were about to be beheaded.

We were taken out of the room into the courtyard adjoining; it was the inner of three courts; and as soon as we were bound, we were again left alone. Parkes told me if my hands were lifted up high behind my back, and they hurried me out, my head would probably be cut off in one of the outer courts. Lifting up the arms when the wrists are bound behind throws the head forward, so that one stroke of the sword can easily sever it from the body.

We said a few sad parting words to each other, for we now considered our deaths as certain. Strange thoughts and feelings enter the mind at such a moment. We believed we had done all we could to compass the escape both of ourselves and those who had been our companions; and I think we were almost more anxious as to the probable future fate of our comrades than we were about our own, which we then considered as fixed beyond all power of reprieve. While we were thus speaking to each other, the soldiers returned, threatening us with their swords and spears; a man suddenly seized my arms, and with one " God bless you" to Parkes, I found myself hurried forward, two or three men on either side of me brandishing their swords. As I passed through the courtyards, I looked forward, and could see through the doors which were opposite to each other, and on to the open country beyond. I was half walking, half running, and had passed nearly through the centre court, when I saw a mandarin coming at full speed towards us. He reached the outer gate at the same moment that I did; exhausted by running, he did not speak, but seizing the man on my left, who had been waving the sword over my head, pushed him away, and throwing his arm over my shoulder, hurried me forward towards a cart close by, into which Parkes and I were thrown. We found the two Frenchmen and the old Sikh in the cart; they were bound like ourselves.

We were driven off at a sharp trot towards Pekin. We again crossed the Pah-li-Chiao bridge, across which crowds of soldiers were now hurrying, as if in retreat.

The agony of that drive I can never forget: it had been bad to bear when we had had our hands free to protect us in some measure from the jolts, but bound as we now were, we were quite powerless to prevent ourselves being thrown backwards and forwards with such violence as at times almost to deprive us of sense. We attempted to steady ourselves by pressing our feet against each other's bodies, but this was too great an exertion to continue long. Occasionally the cart had to go off the paved part, to the side of the road, and if it had not been for these temporary moments of relief, I do not believe any of us could have lived through those hours of terrible torture.

We did our best to conceal what we felt, for several mandarins, attached to the Prince of I's suite, together with a large cavalry escort, rode close in rear of the cart, evidently enjoying and laughing at our sufferings.

One vast encampment appeared to extend along either side of the road, all the way from Tung-chow; in a few places, breastworks seemed partially begun. The dust and heat of the sun were intense, and our throats were parched from exhaustion; they gave us, however, no water, but occasionally an extra pull at the whipcord which bound our wrists, wetting it with water to cause it to shrink. We had asked once for water and were refused; we did not ask again. However, after being about two hours in the cart, they poured some down our throats. After travelling some time, the mandarins seemed to think our cart was too heavily weighted to go fast enough, and removed the two French soldiers into another; the old Sikh, however, we were glad, remained with us. I talked a good deal with him, urging and advising him not to refuse any food that he might be given, but to eat anything he could get, so as to keep up his strength for any opportunity of escape that might offer.

One of the subordinate officials had observed that I had still on my shirt some gold sleeve links, and making some excuse, got into the cart, and tried to steal the buttons; I watched my opportunity, and at a jolt heavier than common, I threw the whole weight of my body on to his hands, jamming them against the edge of the cart. It was a most unwise little display of temper on my part, for he revenged himself by holding my hands raised for some time behind my back, so that at each jolt I expected my shoulders would have been dislocated.

It was dusk before we reached the eastern suburb of Pekin; the streets were crowded, and great curiosity was exhibited to see the prisoners, the people pressing round the cart to such a degree that we could not move beyond a walk. The Tartar soldiers delighted in making the most of their triumph, doubtless wishing the people to think we were but the first instalment of the armies they had promised to annihilate.

As we approached the gate, numbers of women from carts and chairs were gazing curiously and contemptuously at us. We had now been long silent; suddenly I heard Parkes say, "How beautiful!" I asked him what? he said, "That woman;" thinking the beauty must be great indeed that could strike his attention in his then exhausted state, I got my head up to the edge of the cart, and saw the most lovely face, if a face can be lovely, devoid of all feeling and intellectual expression.

We passed through the western gate; the darkness was now rapidly closing in; we were quite exhausted and had again sunk into silence; we traversed street after street; at each moment we thought we should arrive at some temple and there be allowed to rest.

It was quite dark, when suddenly we turned through a gateway into a large court-yard; two or three men with paper lanterns, on which were written Chinese characters, came forward to meet the cart, and I felt Parkes shudder as he read the characters. "This is, indeed, worse," he said, "than I expected, we are in the worst prison in China; we are in the hands of the torturers; this is the Board of Punishments." Those who knew what Chinese tortures were might well shudder at the thought of being in a prison which even by Chinese was the most dreaded of any in the Empire.

The cart was driven up near to some buildings; several men came and lifted Parkes out of the cart, and led him through a door of the nearest house, from which a faint light had glimmered; a quarter of an hour of painful suspense followed; I told Nal-Sing where we were, I told him to keep up his spirits and not fear, and that even if we never escaped, a severe punishment would be inflicted on the Chinese for their conduct towards us—"Fear," replied he, in Hindostanee, "I do not fear; if I do not die to-day I may to-morrow, and I am past sixty, and am I not with you? I do not fear." We presently heard the clank of chains. I raised myself and looked over the side of the cart, and saw Parkes with a heavy chain from his neck being led along supported by two men, another following bearing a lantern. I asked him how he was, he said, "The chains are not very heavy, but I fear they intend to separate us;" he was then taken through a dark doorway out of sight, and I was removed from the cart and led to the same door out of which Parkes had just come; it opened into a small room; on one side was a table, behind which three mandarins were seated. There were various iron implements lying on the table, and the walls were hung with chains and other disagreeable looking instruments, the use of which it was unpleasant too closely to investigate. On one side of the room was a low bench, at each end of which was a small windlass, round which a rope was coiled; the use to which this machine might be applied admitted of no doubt.

On entering, I was shoved down on my knees before the table, a man on either side laying hold of my hair and beard,—a number of questions were asked me, but as I did not understand Chinese, I could not answer them, and each time I failed to reply I got kicked and cuffed. My hat had been knocked off, and feeling the importance, if possible, of regaining it, for it was probable I might be greatly exposed to the sun, I made a movement to rise and get it, but was immediately knocked down and kicked. An iron collar was then secured round my neck, with a heavy chain extending to my feet. I again made signs to regain my hat, and, as much to my surprise as pleasure, a man picked it up and put it on my head. I was then led away to a courtyard, where I found Parkes seated on a bench, having irons fixed on his ankles, —they would not allow us to speak. Double irons were then attached to my ankles, the chain between being only about three inches long, and this was passed through one of the links of the chain from my neck; we were then led away in different directions.

It appeared to be too probable we should never meet again, and my heart sank as I said "God bless you, Parkes," and the sound of his chains as he passed through the further courts grew fainter and fainter; while together, we could support each other, and this had been an inexpressible comfort in the trying hours through which we had passed.

Two men assisted me to walk (the ankle chain being so short I could only shuffle along). I passed through several passages and courts, and at last found myself in rather a larger one than the others. On the right of this court, as we entered, there were some sheds and other buildings, evidently used as a kind of kitchen, and on the left a small Buddhist temple; along the whole of the further side of the court, opposite the door at which we had entered, there extended a long, dark, barn-like building. The door which opened into the court was closed, but there was a gleam of light shining through the chinks. My gaolers went up to the door, and gave three heavy blows, crying out at the same time. A most unearthly yell from the inside was the reply; the door was thrown open, and I found myself in the presence of, and surrounded by, as savage a lot of half-naked demons as I had ever beheld; they were nearly all the lowest class of criminals, imprisoned for murder and the most serious offences. There were about fifty in all, of whom some eighteen or twenty were chained like myself, but with far lighter irons. A few of the prisoners were better dressed than the others.

My arrival was for the gaol a most exciting event, and it roused them all. The heat and closeness being excessive, few had more clothes on than trousers, or a girdle round their middle; they crowded round, gazing with curiosity at me.

On one side of the room, running its whole length, was a wooden bench, extending about eight feet from the wall, sloping a little towards it; this was the sleeping place; chains hung down from several of the beams, reaching nearly to the bench, with the use of which I was soon to be made practically acquainted. The gaoler, as soon as I entered, pinioned my elbows, my wrists were still bound,—I had lost all sensation in my left hand—having however to fix handcuffs on my wrists, they in a little time released the cords; this was an immense relief. Just as they were about to clasp the irons on my wrists, they observed the ring on my finger, which had escaped the notice of those who had searched me in Juilin's camp. It excited the cupidity of one of the gaolers, who finding in the then swollen state of my hand that it could not be got off, rubbed and sucked my finger in his mouth, munching it gently with his teeth until it was sufficiently softened to get the ring off—and he was welcome to it, for I believe the measures he took to restore the circulation saved me my hand.

My hands were then handcuffed, the short chain which connected them being passed through a link in the one which descended from my neck to my feet.

I was parched with thirst, and determined to ask for some water—I knew just sufficient Chinese for that; to my delight, instead of water they brought me a cup of tea, for even in this gaol it stood always ready for the use of the gaolers; I was also given a piece of bread. I was then laid down on the bench which I have described, with my feet towards the wall, directly under one of the chains hanging from the beam above; to this the chain round my neck was attached, and I was thus only able to lie flat on my back, and even this was painful with my elbows pinioned.

After this chain was made fast, they ceased to speak to me, and truly glad I was at being left to my own thoughts. I was utterly exhausted, and in five minutes fell into a heavy sleep. I awoke about two hours afterwards, chilled, and shivering. That was a most wretched waking;—so crowded was the prison, that my neighbours on either side touched me,—the one on my right hand feeling me shaking with cold, drew his tattered, vermin-eaten rug over me—and I was thankful.

CHAPTER XI.

MY PRISON LIFE.

A LITTLE before daylight the following morning I was awoke by the stir in the prison; for a few moments I could not realise my position; in the hope that I was dreaming I closed my eyes, but the clank of the chains as I slightly moved quickly recalled me to a full sense of my position. I raised my arms as high as the rope which pinioned my elbows would admit, to see the shadow of my manacled wrists on the wall,—a few feeble oil lamps giving just sufficient light for this purpose. As I moved I felt a heavy hand on my chest, and for the first time noticed that a man, one of the prisoners, was seated on the ground, near my head, keeping watch over me; I afterwards discovered three prisoners were appointed to perform this duty, and one or other of these men never moved a yard from me during the whole period of my imprisonment in this gaol.

At sunrise, there was a loud shout outside, and the door being thrown open, those prisoners who were not chained to the walls or beams went into the courtyard.

Although there were many in chains, there were only two besides myself secured to bolts let into the walls or rafters. In about a quarter of an hour after the door had been opened the gaolers returned and undid the padlocks by which we were fastened, and allowed us also into the yard.

By daylight the court appeared to me smaller than it had done the previous night. The prison occupied, as I have already described, one side of the enclosure, the only entrance into which, was by a small door in the wall opposite, which was of considerable height. On the right of the prison was the small Buddhist temple or shrine which I have already mentioned; and on the left, a few wretched sheds which served as a kitchen for the gaolers and some of the prisoners who possessed exclusive privileges. This was but one of many similar prisons within the precincts of the Board of Punishments.

The gaolers and prisoners evinced great curiosity at my appearance, crowding round to examine my clothes, jack-boots, and skin. My acquaintance with Asiatic character taught me that not only my comfort while in prison would depend, but possibly my future safety, upon the position which from the first I should assume, and the deference I might be able to exact, both from my gaolers and my fellow-sufferers. My being unable to speak Chinese made me feel all the more the necessity of supplying, by my manner, my inability to communicate with them by words. When, therefore, both the officers of the prison and the convicted criminals began touching my hands, face, and hair, I at once made them understand their curiosity and familiarity were displeasing to me, and moved, as well as my chains would admit, towards a small wooden bench, the only one within the prison, on which at the time two men were seated. I motioned them to rise, and, to make my meaning fully understood, at the same time gently shoved them; they instantly rose, their faces expressing the utmost astonishment. I seated myself on the bench, and signed that I wished the space in front of me to be kept clear. Two men, however, whether intentionally or otherwise I could not say, sat down on the ground close before me, but upon going up to them and touching them with my foot, they immediately moved away. Not wishing to tax their obedience too severely, I then signed to the prisoners to be seated on either side, upon which they all squatted upon the ground. During the three or four minutes this occupied, not a word was spoken; they were all silent, partly with astonishment, and partly with curiosity, watching what I should do next; but from that moment I was treated with the greatest deference and respect by my fellow-prisoners, and I never went into the yard without the bench being at once brought for me to sit down upon, and the kindly feeling they always afterwards exhibited was very touching. Some of these poor fellows had friends outside who occasionally managed to have conveyed to them a few cakes or apples, but hungry and nearly starving as they were, they always made an offering of their food to me before they thought of eating it themselves.

The discipline of the prison was in itself not very strict, and had it not been for the starvation, the pain arising from the cramped position in which the chains and ropes retained the arms and legs, with the heavy drag of the iron collar on the bones of the spine, and the creeping vermin that infested every place, together with the occasional beatings and tortures which the prisoners were from time to time taken away for a few hours to endure, —returning with bleeding legs and bodies, and so weak as to be scarce able to crawl,— there was no very great hardship to be endured. Every morning about sunrise the door was opened from the outside by the principal officials of the prison, who announced their approach by loud shouts; all the prisoners who were allowed the full use of their arms and legs, hurried into the yard, and were allowed to walk up and down, and occasionally they succeeded in obtaining a little water with which to wash. The more serious offenders, of whom I was considered to be the chief, were allowed out, from a quarter, to half an hour later. Here the prisoners remained until, as far as I could calculate, near seven o'clock, when with the exception of those in chains, they were all locked up, while we more unfortunate individuals were drawn up in line in the yard; two men then entered, bearing between them a large tub full of boiled millet; they were accompanied by two subordinate mandarins to superintend the distribution of this prison fare. This was the only food allowed by Government regulation, and is only given to those of the class in which I was placed, namely, to the worst class of criminal and political offenders—each prisoner being given a good-sized bowlful. Millet possesses very little nourishment, and the quantity allowed is only sufficient to support life. As soon as the distribution was finished, the mandarins withdrew, and the other prisoners were again admitted into the yard. There appeared to be three dietary scales, the millet, or the worst scale, being provided at the expense of the Government; the two others at the expense of one or more of the prisoners, who are allowed in this manner to work off a portion of their sentence by providing food, with the assistance of their friends outside, for those whom the prison authorities may direct should be better fed.

When I was first imprisoned there were about forty-eight prisoners in my ward; nineteen of these besides myself were in chains;

about fifteen, by length of imprisonment, had been relieved of their chains, and had consequently been promoted to better food, while the remaining thirteen were imprisoned, either on suspicion of having committed some offence, or for having refused to pay some exaction levied by the government. Some of these latter were really well fed, many of them being able to contribute towards their own keep. Those released from their chains were most of them criminal offenders; they were fed on rice, two, occasionally three small bowls of it in the day, sometimes with a little vegetable, and once or twice I saw about an ounce of chopped meat given. I was glad to find that I was placed on the rice diet, which had perhaps a degree more nourishment in it than the millet. About eight o'clock each morning I was taken inside and chained up to my beam, and given a bowl of rice. I was generally let into the yard again, as far as I could guess about eleven, and permitted to remain there until between three and four o'clock, when I was again chained up, and given my dinner, which was the same as my breakfast, with, at rare intervals, the addition of a little cabbage; after that I was allowed into the yard before being locked up for the night, which was always a little after sunset. The prisoners who were appointed to watch my movements, used to take every morning and night a small rag, and carefully examine and wash my neck and wrists where the ropes and irons had galled my skin. At first I was at a loss to know the reason of their care, but I soon became aware of the fearful consequences which they dreaded might ensue if this precaution had been neglected. There is a small maggot which appears to infest all Chinese prisons; the earth at the depth of a few inches swarms with them; they are the scourge most dreaded by every poor prisoner. Few enter a Chinese gaol who have not on their bodies or limbs some wounds, either inflicted by blows to which they have been subjected, or caused by the manner in which they have been bound; the instinct of the insect to which I allude, appears to lead them direct to these wounds. Bound and helpless, the poor wretch cannot save himself from their approach, although he knows full well that if they once succeed in reaching his lacerated skin, there is the certainty of a fearful, lingering, and agonising death before him. My right-hand neighbour on the bench, where we all slept at night, was dying from the inroads of these insects; his suffering was great, and the relief his fellow-prisoners could afford was of no avail. The crowded state of the gaol brought me in such close contact at night with this poor fellow, that our heads rested on the same block of wood not a foot apart. The thought, as I lay pinioned and ironed, unable to move, during the long, dark nights, that his fate at any moment might be my own, was at times difficult to bear with calmness and with that outward appearance of indifference which it was necessary I should maintain.

On *Wednesday*, the 19th of September, the first day of my imprisonment, the astonishment and curiosity of my companions had scarcely begun to subside when loud cries in the outer courts announced the approach of a mandarin of high rank; all the prisoners were hurried into the prison, and I was chained up again to the beam. After a little time the gaolers, handling me roughly, led me into the court yard. I there found three mandarins, one of whom I thought I recognised, but I could not recall where I had seen him. I afterwards ascertained that he was the President of the Board of Punishments. These mandarins were accompanied by a number of attendants. I was pushed rudely forward and forced upon my knees, then ensued a tiresome examination, of which I did not understand a word. After a quarter of an hour spent in vain efforts to teach me Chinese, the lesson being assisted by kicks and cuffs, the mandarins left; during the day I had three similar visits from other officials, the President of the Board of Punishments coming once more; his manner and behaviour were very brutal. I had unfortunately endeavoured to ask where Parkes was, but my attempt to do so led me into trouble, for they immediately imagined I knew more of the language than I had acknowledged.

In the afternoon I asked the gaoler, partly by signs and partly by a few words, to get back a book which had been taken from me the previous night. I did not know whether he understood me or not.

I was not sorry when this anxious day drew towards a close, and I could lie down and be at least quiet, but even in this I was disappointed, for very soon after the doors of the prison were locked and sealed (they were always sealed on the outside with paper bearing the official seal), the gaolers, who are locked up at night with the prisoners, lit some small lamps, and began to play various games amongst themselves, and with those prisoners who were allowed the liberty of moving about, but in about a couple of hours the talking and laughing gradually ceased; all the lamps, except the night ones, were extinguished, and I was left to my own painful thoughts.

Thursday, 20th. — To my surprise the gaoler brought me this forenoon the book which I yesterday asked should be returned.

A number of mandarins again visited me during the day. I was kept at times ten and fifteen minutes on my knees.

Friday, 21st.—For fear of losing the reckoning of the days of the month, I got a piece of mortar out of the wall, and wrote down the day of the week, and date, on a smooth stone; I also took every opportunity I could of writing my name on the wall, so that in the event of my being removed, or anything happening to me, if the army took Pekin and search was made, it might be known I had been confined here. I felt the importance of this, for after the capture of Canton in 1858, I remembered having been one of a party that searched the prisons in that town to discover, if possible, some trace of several Englishmen who had been captured at Whampoo and other places during the war. If we could have ascertained with certainty that they had been in any one of the gaols we could have followed up the clue, by holding the officers of the prison responsible until the fate of the missing men had been discovered. As it was, the officials denied all knowledge of ever having seen the persons of whom we were in search.

Mandarins still came to look and stare at me, as if I was some strange wild beast, and I dare say I was not very unlike one in appearance with my hair and beard matted and uncombed, and my clothes dirty and torn from repeated kneelings and draggings on the ground.

This evening when the prison was closed, I endeavoured to learn a few Chinese words; the gaolers became interested and began teaching me to count, and the names of various articles; and the result was they chained me up an hour later than usual.

Saturday, 22nd.—What with a few words and signs I fancied I was able to establish some sort of communication with the gaolers and prisoners; seeing one of the gaolers writing, I made signs to be allowed the brush and Indian ink which he was using; he at once gave them together with some paper. I thought he might probably be flattered if I attempted a sketch of him; he rejoiced in the name of "Cow," and was as ugly a specimen of humanity as can well be imagined. My likeness was, I fear, too correct, for while it was received with a shout of applause and roars of laughter by the other gaolers and prisoners, Cow was so incensed that he immediately hurried me into the prison and chained me up to my beam, as a punishment for my indiscretion. In the evening, after the door was locked, the other gaolers made Cow release me, and resumed their lessons in Chinese; they also gave me the brush and Indian ink again, and I began the diary from which I now write, on the inside lining of my hat.

Sunday, 23rd.—The days pass wearily by. Only the official mandarins of the prison now visit me, I can hear nothing of Parkes; I sometimes think of attempting by a sudden shout to attract his attention if he is within hearing so that he might reply, and have thought of singing "God save the Queen" or "Rule Britannia."

The quantity of rice I get does not suffice to keep off the cravings of hunger, but it is better food than the millet diet, on which the other poor fellows are fed; some of them to-day received a present of a few pears and cakes; they came and offered them to me, and would not be satisfied until I had broken a small piece off a biscuit and eaten it.

Monday, 24th.—Each day hoping almost against hope, I tried to ascertain if our army was advancing, and if it was to be peace or war; either my signs could not be understood or the gaolers were ignorant of what was passing outside, probably both, for I could get no information.

Tuesday, 25th.—Picking up a few more words of Chinese.

I determined to-day to try "God save the Queen," but had scarcely commenced when I found I had no heart to go on; the gaolers and prisoners were greatly astonished at my sudden shout. I afterwards learnt from Parkes that he had made a similar attempt to attract my attention, but had stopped from the same cause.

This evening I made a fresh endeavour to ascertain the position of affairs outside. I got the brush, Indian ink, and some paper, and drew a figure which I intended to represent a mandarin, and another figure intended to represent Lord Elgin, seated together at a table in the act of applying a seal to a document lying between them, the official seal in China being the confirmatory act that is required to be attached to all agreements to give them validity. By the side of this I drew an English soldier running a Chinaman through the body with his bayonet. I intended my pictures to represent peace and war, but as they were anything but artistic drawings, I had some doubts whether they even took in my meaning; however on my pointing first to one and then to the other, they all selected the peaceable picture, but whether this was only an expression of their own individual preference for sitting at a table, to being run through the body I could not determine; I at all events tried to believe they meant that the Convention would be signed in a few days.

Wednesday, 26th.—I was told this evening that Hang-ki had been with Parkes—there had been much excitement in the prison all day. Pie, the head-gaoler, was very uncivil, and locked me up for some hours sooner than usual, and when I asked for water took no notice; I repeated my request, and received no answer; it might have been well if I had said nothing further; the prisoner in charge of me tried to stop my speaking, but I called again to the gaoler by name, and in an authoritative manner ordered him to bring me some water. Pie then jumped up, and calling to the other gaolers to assist him, so tightened my chain to the beam that I was partly suspended by my neck and feet, the iron collar round my neck acting as a halter. I was left this way for the night—the prisoner on duty occasionally lifting me to ease the pressure on my neck and throat when he saw me choking. From weakness and exhaustion, I kept dozing off to sleep, but I could not have lasted much longer, when the first streaks of daylight began to make their way into the prison. In about half-an-hour later my chain was loosed. As soon as I had recovered sufficiently to speak, I again called to Pie; he came at once; I this time, instead of asking for water, told him to bring me a cup of tea, which, somewhat to my surprise, he immediately went and brought from the stand where it always stood ready for the gaolers' use, day and night.

Thursday, 27th.—From my last night's treatment, and the gaoler's manner all yesterday, I felt something important had happened, and that danger threatened. By signs I was given to understand negotiations of some kind were going forward.

Friday, 28th.—No change, all my calculations at fault to account for the delay in the advance of our army. A few days ago while sitting inside the prison, a prisoner whom I had often noticed from his dispirited and unhappy appearance, came and sat down by me. After looking in my face for some time, he suddenly addressed to me a few words in Persian—naming, God, Jesus, Mecca, Medina, Mahomed, Persia, &c., but when I attempted any connected sentence, I found that the few words he had spoken had exhausted his vocabulary; he then went to the kitchen, and having procured a piece of charred stick wrote on the wall in Persian characters the words he had repeated; beyond this he had no acquaintance with the language, but upon my also writing the same words, on the wall, as well as my chained wrists would admit, he was greatly pleased. By signs and a very few Chinese words I had learnt, I ascertained, or fancied I did so, something of his history. I gathered that he was on his journey home after transacting some mercantile business in Pekin when he was arrested as a political offender; the part of the country where he resided being at the time in a state of rebellion, and, having no friends in Pekin who could assist him with money, and being unable himself to pay the amount which would have purchased his release, he had been kept two years in prison. The day before yesterday he had been suddenly summoned to appear before the Council of the Board of Punishments. In an hour's time he returned, his whole face lit up with joy; it was evident that he was to be discharged, he hastily packed up the few rags he possessed, in a silk handkerchief, and sat waiting for the arrival of the official order for his release. Hour after hour passed, the joy gradually, as the time advanced, faded from his face, and was succeeded by a look of the most anxious care. It was not until near sunset he was again sent for, he was only absent a few minutes, but his bitter grief on his return showed too evidently that at the last moment his pardon had been withheld; and overcome with sorrow he threw himself down alongside me on our hard wooden couch, and gave way to his despair. Poor fellow! I could do little to comfort him; the false hope into which he had been deluded, made his imprisonment all the more painful to bear. This forenoon he was again sent for; he went, but not with the same hopeful look as before; in a few minutes he returned radiant with delight, and seizing me by my hands pressed them to his heart, then, catching up his bundle which he had never untied, hurried out a free man; and before night I trust the poor fellow was well on his homeward road.

Saturday, 29*th*.—In the forenoon my chief attendant prisoner gave me to understand that something was occurring affecting me personally, and that my chains were to be taken off. I attempted to school myself to bear the disappointment if he was misleading me, or in case I misunderstood his meaning, but in the afternoon the loud cries which always heralded the approach of a mandarin of high rank, told me that I was likely to receive a visit on the result of which my future fate would depend. The gaolers hurried about and made the prisoners fall back in a line behind me, and I remained seated on the small bench which I always appropriated to myself. The door leading into the courtyard was suddenly thrown open, and Hang-ki walked hurriedly in; I had not seen him since the evening previous to our capture, when we had met on friendly and equal terms. I saw at once that there was to be some change in my treatment, for although I rose as Hang-ki entered, the gaoler did not lead me up to force me on my knees, which had hitherto always been the case, even to the most paltry of the official mandarins; but as I stood chained and bound in front of him, Hang-ki walked quickly up to me, spoke rapidly in Chinese to the gaolers, seizing at the same time with one hand the iron collar round my neck, while with the other he beckoned that it should be removed. The gaolers hastened to obey the order, and in a few minutes I was able to stretch my aching limbs. Hang-ki then taking me by my hand would have led me away, but I was not prepared to part from those—villains though they might be—who had in my hour of trial shown me kindness and sympathy; therefore, drawing my hand away, I walked up to the prisoners, and beginning on the right of the line passed down and bade farewell to each man by repeating the usual Chinese term, chin-chin, —Hang-ki chafing with indignation and impatience at being kept waiting. But although the majority of the prisoners were perhaps as great criminals as the world could produce, I knew them only as sharers of my sufferings, and as the authors of many touching acts of most disinterested kindness. When I rejoined him, Hang-ki, taking me again by the hand, led me through several courts and passages until we reached a small room, where I was shortly joined by Parkes. The Chinese closed the door, and left us alone; and I will also close the door on the first few moments of our meeting.

CHAPTER XII.

OUR PRISON LIFE.

Up to the moment of our meeting I did not know whether this was to be our final release, or whether it was to be merely a change in our prison treatment. I learnt at once from Parkes that it was only the latter; he told me that for some days the Chinese authorities had been urging him to write to Lord Elgin to withdraw the army, the Imperial Government being ignorantly persuaded that the threat of putting us to death in the event of a non-compliance with their request, would deter Lord Elgin from attempting to enforce terms repugnant to the wishes of the Emperor, and that to bring about a result so favourable to themselves it only required Lord Elgin to be satisfied on this point, and for Parkes to request him to abate his demands. Notwithstanding the absurdity of the request and the ignorance it displayed, Parkes thought he might take advantage of their evident anxiety that he should write to Lord Elgin to secure better treatment for himself and the rest of the prisoners, he therefore said he declined to write a word while he was treated like a common criminal, and that if they insisted on his writing he would date it from the Board of Punishments; to this they greatly objected, for they felt there was but small probability of Lord Elgin's believing no undue influence had been employed to enforce the writing of the letter if he learnt where we were confined. The following day, therefore, Hang-ki told Parkes that if he would consent to write a letter in the manner desired by the Chinese Government he would be removed to a small temple in the north of the city, which had been prepared for his reception. Parkes expressed his willingness to comply with these terms on condition that I was to accompany him. When he made this demand he was uncertain whether I was still alive, but as he saw at once from Hang-ki's manner that I was, Parkes pressed this condition more strongly, stating that as I had been commissioned with him to negotiate with the Chinese Commissioners my consent was necessary to the proposed letter, and he positively refused to write it unless I was associated with him in the change of treatment.

After a strong remonstrance against the delay this would occasion, as I could not be removed without the consent of Prince Kung, the Emperor's brother, who had been appointed Regent during the Emperor's absence in Tartary, Hang-ki at last consented to take the necessary steps for obtaining an order for my transfer to better quarters and treatment; this occurred the day previous to the one on which we were brought together.

Parkes had only time to explain hurriedly to me the position of affairs when Hang-ki returned. We were then led into the outer court, where we found two covered carts, very different from the one in which we had travelled to Pekin; these were "carriage carts," fitted up inside with cushions and pillows, to prevent the roughness of the roads being too severely felt, which was very necessary, for they possessed the rudest apologies for springs. A very fine body of

Tartar cavalry were in attendance to escort us. We wished to travel in the same cart, but this was not allowed. As soon as we were seated Hang-ki mounted a rough handsome Tartar horse, of which he seemed to be in some fear, and took command; two of our old gaolers were attached to each of us, to act now not only in their old, but in a new capacity, viz., as our servants, and seated themselves on the shafts of the carts. We moved along the west side of the town, in some places skirting the walls of the Imperial or Inner City, until we approached the northern wall, when we turned to the eastward and stopped at a temple not far from the An-ting, the easternmost of the two north gates of Pekin. We entered the outer court, and as soon as the gates were shut we were taken out of the carts, and led through two enclosed yards. Opening into the inner court, we found a building very comfortably prepared for our use. A temple facing this building was occupied by our escort, and a picked guard of twenty Tartar cavalry (one of whom stood six feet seven inches, and strong in proportion) was placed over us. These men were very civil and obliging during the whole period of our confinement in this temple.

It was amusing to observe the gaolers, who had but yesterday lorded it over us with almost despotic power, now mild and submissive to every word. Pie, my friend who had made me feel his power, was now as gentle as a lamb.

In our rooms we found tubs and plenty of water; the luxury of a thorough good wash after all we had passed through is indescribable; the sad part was, however, returning into our dirty clothes, which had lively recollections connected with them.

As soon as we were dressed, the dinner was announced. It was brought from a neighbouring restaurant; and came in large wooden boxes, not very dissimilar to those used by Gunter and other confectioners in London. The dinner consisted of sixteen moderate sized dishes, thirty-two smaller ones, and various kinds of soups. Pieces of mutton, fowl, turkey, unknown gelatinous substances, and a variety of other meats, filled the larger dishes,—with vegetables dressed in different ways; and in the smaller ones were pickles, small pieces of salt fish, and various kinds of relish to be eaten with the more substantial part of the entertainment. All the dishes were excellently cooked and exceedingly good. What a dinner to set before two half-starved men! but, alas! the very effects of our semi-starvation had produced such nausea and faintness at the sight of the food that we could not touch it. They had, however, not confined the feast to eatables,—there were several kinds of wine. Some made from rice and warmed, was rather good, and we found it enabled us to eat a little. Parkes said it would never do to allow a similar dinner to be sent to us daily, as some unfortunate fellow, possibly Hang-ki, would be called on by the Government to pay the cost of our entertainment out of his own pocket, and as he would soon tire of providing us with such abundance, he might possibly, by inserting some unpleasant ingredient in the food, relieve himself from the necessity of furnishing it any longer. Parkes therefore begged our dinner should not exceed eight dishes for the future.

We had scarcely finished dinner when a message came from Hang-ki to say he would call in ten minutes. On arrival, he at once claimed from Parkes the fulfilment of his promise to write to Lord Elgin. Parkes acquiesced, and said that as the Imperial Government had kept its promise to him and had now evinced an intention of treating us in a manner more suitable to our position, he would write the letter they required. Hang-ki then dictated a letter which Parkes wrote in Chinese; it was to the effect that Prince Kung, brother of the Emperor, had been appointed High Commissioner to settle all foreign differences; that he was a man of great ability and high attainments; that our army was not to advance nearer to Pekin, but that there should be a conference to discuss and arrange the terms of a convention to be concluded between the Emperor and the Allied Sovereigns, &c., &c. When the letter was finished Parkes suggested to Hang-ki, that it would have more weight with Lord Elgin if my opinion in favour of the course recommended could be stated, but that unfortunately I did not write Chinese, and that therefore the only way of signifying my approval would be by writing a few lines across the letter. Hang-ki at once gladly assented, feeling sure he had the means of ascertaining through the mandarin Hwang, whom I have already mentioned at the capture of the Taku forts, what I might write. Being also aware of this, I wrote in Hindostanee, although in English characters:—"This letter is written by order of the Chinese Government.—H. B. LOCH." If it was ever shown to Hwang, he probably, not liking to acknowledge his inability to read what I had written, invented something for the occasion, as the letter was forwarded. It was the first intimation Lord Elgin received of our being alive, and most useful it proved, for hitherto not knowing what had been our fate he had been afraid, when writing, to allude to the prisoners except in general terms, but after the receipt of this letter he always mentioned Parkes and myself by name, and told the Chinese Government that he held it responsible for our lives.

Sunday, 30th.—A present of fruit arrived early this morning from Prince Kung. Parkes had a long conversation with the bearer, who was Hang-ki's confidential servant; we tried to learn something of what was going on outside,—if there had been any more fighting since our capture, and if our army was near Pekin,—but, whether intentionally or through ignorance, he would give us no information.

Shortly after he had left, Hang-ki called, accompanied by the Commander-in-Chief of the garrison of Pekin (which at this time was held to number over eighty thousand men), and by several other mandarins. The conversation principally turned upon the certain ruin which would overtake the Allied armies if the Ambassadors persisted in their demands, and the necessity of our submitting, without giving further trouble, to the orders of the Emperor. They did not remain above half an hour.

During the afternoon we were not disturbed by any more visitors. We walked for some hours in the courtyard, talking over the probabilities of release, and the far more probable failure of any attempt at peaceful negotiations.

Monday, October 1st.—Last night we were both very ill, but this morning are much better. Hang-ki called early, and said if we wished to send for any clothes we could do so, as he was sending in a messenger with a flag of truce with a letter to Lord Elgin. It was evidently Hang-ki's desire that we should avail ourselves of this opportunity, to urge on Lord Elgin the adoption of a more conciliatory policy; Hang-ki also wanted a meeting to be arranged between Mr. Wade and himself. We at once accepted the offer, and Parkes was allowed to write a few lines requesting some things to be sent, and also to arrange the meeting Hang-ki desired.

Tuesday, 2nd.—The Manchus who formed our guard could not speak Chinese well, and Parkes was therefore unable to gain much from them respecting the position of affairs, even if they had been willing to impart the information.

A present of a small package of tea was sent this morning by Prince Kung. It was of a very rare kind, only grown for the use of the Imperial family, and was of wonderful delicacy and flavour; its arrival caused quite an excitement among our servants and guard. Hang-ki called with several of the mandarins in the afternoon, but brought no news.

Feeling, during the long evenings, it was necessary to do something to divert, if possible, our thoughts from dwelling too constantly on our position, we manufactured a backgammon-board out of a cushion belonging to one of the chairs, by pasting on it pieces of paper cut in the proper form; and for men we got some copper cash from our servants, distinguishing the white from the black by covering them with paper. Our inventive genius was greatly at fault to discover a substitute for dice, but at last we hit on a plan of numbering six pieces of paper in duplicate, which we drew two at a time from a hat. In this way we passed an hour or so of the long anxious evenings.

Wednesday, 3*rd*.—A lovely, cloudless day. It gave us an intense longing to be free, and made us envy each bird or insect that flew or buzzed over the walls of our courtyard.

About noon, Hang-ki and several mandarins called. Hang-ki's servant brought some clothes, and also a letter from Wade to Parkes, which told us that several letters had passed between Lord Elgin and Prince Kung with reference to the terms on which the Allies would be ready to negotiate; but that owing to the repeated evasion on the part of the Chinese, the Allied armies had advanced close to Pekin, and intended to shell the town if there was any further delay in complying with the Ambassadors' demands. Parkes read this letter to Hang-ki, and a long unsatisfactory conversation ensued. All the mandarins were obstinate, and ignorantly ignored the danger in which their procrastination and falsehood involved them. As Hang-ki persisted in making light of it, Parkes at last said, the destruction of Pekin and the overthrow of the Dynasty will be owing to the folly of those who advise at the present juncture any but the most straightforward policy. We felt, although he would not admit it, that Hang-ki was really very much alarmed. He was the only mandarin amongst them of very high rank who had ever been brought into personal contact with Europeans; he had been for several years at Canton, and had had much to do with Parkes at various times; indeed, for a short period he had been detained as a prisoner, and Parkes frequently reminded him of this, and contrasted the manner in which he had then been treated, with the way in which the Chinese Government had behaved to us. He was pretty well acquainted with the character of English officials, and knew their word was to be trusted. On one occasion, when a mandarin, hearing Parkes remark that he would not demand redress against those who had ill-used us, observed,—" It is all very well to say that now, but if you were once free, you might take quite a different view of the matter," Hang-ki at once interposed, and said,—" No! I have some experience of the English, and they have a habit, and a very curious one, of speaking the truth."

After sitting with us nearly two hours, the mandarins rose to go. Parkes had written to Wade acknowledging the receipt of the clothes and his letter. The misfortune is, he wrote, the Chinese will not believe in their danger, nor that Lord Elgin will act up to his threats. I consider our course nearly run. While Parkes had been writing and conversing with Hang-ki and the others, I had been carefully examining the clothes which had been sent, as we thought it possible some communication might be concealed in them. I observed an embroidered evening shirt and a handkerchief with an embroidered monogram, both curious articles of wearing apparel, it struck me, to send to two men in our position; so, while Parkes was engaging Hang-ki's attention, I took the handkerchief to the window, and found, neatly worked round the embroidery, a few sentences in Hindostanee, to the effect that the siege guns were in position, and that the bombardment was to open the third day, and wishing us, if possible, to communicate our exact position in the city to Lord Elgin. As soon as I told Parkes the information required, he ascertained, without creating suspicion, the name of the temple in which we were confined, and the names of the streets in our immediate neighbourhood, and when writing to Wade he dated his letter accordingly.

As soon as we were alone, we had again a thorough look through all the clothes, and discovered some similar sentences to those I had already found embroidered on the handkerchief, worked on the shirt.

We felt that a few days would now decide our fate; and with a knowledge of their procrastinating character we had but slight hope; Hang-ki's parting words being—" The first shot that is fired will be the signal for your execution."

Thursday, 4*th*.—Anxiously calculating the

day on which, according to the writing on the shirt and handkerchief, the fire would open. We thought it had probably been written on the 2nd; this would make to-morrow the third day.

At about 11.30 Hang-ki called; he was soon followed by some of the principal mandarins, both civil and military, within Pekin; several we had not seen before. We suspected that some of them had called merely to taste the flavour of the Imperial tea which had been sent to us, for the custom is to serve each visitor with tea, the servants bringing in relays,—no sooner is one cup finished than it is replaced by a full one. With such a heavy run on it, the small quantity did not last more than a couple of days, but it was highly appreciated, for even very few of these great mandarins had ever before had an opportunity of tasting it. We were told a very small quantity of it was grown, and that in only one particular district.

Hang-ki told us he had sent Parkes' letter to Wade, and that letters had also been written to Lord Elgin requesting him to name a place and time for a conference, and that he hoped to-morrow to receive a reply to this communication. We, however, felt we could not depend on the truth of this statement.

Parkes has endeavoured repeatedly to ascertain what is the fate of the other prisoners, but can learn nothing; indeed, so little will Hang-ki say on the subject, that we sometimes think they must have been allowed, under the flag of truce, to pass in safety through the Chinese army, or that they effected their escape in some other way. Hang-ki avoids the subject, and will only give general answers.

Friday, 5th.—As this morning at daybreak was the time we expected the bombardment to commence, we listened anxiously as the first streaks of light began to find their way into our room; but as minute after minute passed, and at last an hour, and yet no sound, we began to have some belief in the probability of the meeting which Hang-ki told us yesterday had been requested by Prince Kung. We feel that either to-day or to-morrow our fate must be decided, and yet we are glad that the crisis has arrived; and although a failure of negotiations will, we know, terminate our existence, we cannot help thinking also what an effect it will have on the destinies of China, for we feel sure an attack on Pekin will destroy the present Dynasty, and possibly plunge the Empire into anarchy for years. The thought of this is more distressing to poor Parkes than our own position.

We had a message early this morning from Hang-ki, saying he would call if possible this afternoon, but could not do so sooner. The object of his daily visit, and that of the other mandarins, appears to be the hope that during the long conversations some suggestions may be made by Parkes to guide and assist them in their conduct. The conversation, on whatever subject it may commence, always concludes with the question,—"What do you advise being done?" At first, Parkes' answer could only be, that we were ignorant of all that had occurred since our capture, and that unless they told us what communications had passed between the Ambassadors and the Chinese Government, and the present position of the Allied armies, it was impossible for us to offer an opinion; but if they would place us in possession of the true state of affairs, we would do our best to advise.

This they always evaded doing, only urging the more strenuously that we should point out some way of bringing Lord Elgin to reason, and making him abate what they called his unreasonable demands. Such conversations occurred daily; they nearly always ended in vague threats of violence to us personally. On more than one occasion, Parkes pointed out the risk which they incurred from their procrastinating conduct,—that it materially increased the difficulties of their position, and was the line of policy the most likely to force Lord Elgin to adopt the extreme measure of destroying Pekin, and deposing the reigning Dynasty. On one occasion, about the 1st inst., Hang-ki explained the difficulty that existed to re-opening negotiations by a meeting between commissioners appointed by Lord Elgin and those appointed by the Imperial Commissioners; for he said,—"After the way in which you have been treated, none of your people will trust us, and none of ours are willing to place themselves in the power of your army, for fear of being detained as hostages." This was so evidently true, that Parkes, feeling how important it was to re-open communication between the Chinese Authorities and the Allied Ambassadors, said, the difficulty named by Hang-ki might be at once removed by sending back all the prisoners. The mandarins received this proposal with such ridicule that Parkes declined to converse further on the subject until they apologised, which they at once did. He then suggested, "You can either send Loch or myself, the one remaining a hostage for the other's return in the event of the negotiations failing to bring about a satisfactory settlement of existing differences." This proposal Hang-ki said they would consider. He then went on to discuss the question of any of those captured ever being released, for he said, "When you tell Lord Elgin of the manner in which you have been treated, he will revenge your sufferings on us, and on the people." Parkes replied it was impossible for him to say what steps Lord Elgin might think it right to take to punish an outrage so gross as the violation of a flag of truce, but he could speak for ourselves, and could state, that in the event of our being released we would not demand any punishment being inflicted on account of what had occurred to us individually, provided the Chinese Government continued to treat us properly. This was all that passed on that occasion. The day following we were informed that the Chinese Government could not entertain Parkes' suggestion, so we did not at that time again allude to the subject, as it was always our endeavour to show a perfect indifference to all they might do or say to us individually, merely pointing out how delay endangered their own safety.

In the afternoon Hang-ki called; he was alone, and appeared distressed and anxious. After talking on indifferent subjects for a short time, he said,—" I have seen Wade to-day." He then told us the meeting, which they had written yesterday to request, had been arranged for this forenoon, and had taken place at a village a few miles in advance of the Allied armies; that Wade had consented to meet him alone, none of the other Chinese Commissioners daring to accompany him for fear of being detained as hostages for our safety. Hang-ki then said that Wade had brought a letter from Lord Elgin, in which, instead of lowering his demands, they were raised and made more impossible to concede than ever; that Lord Elgin now required that one of the gates of Pekin should be surrendered and garrisoned by the Allied troops until the Treaty and proposed Convention were ratified. This and other conditions, on his return from the interview, Hang-ki had laid before the council intrusted under Prince Kung with the government of the Empire; there had been a long and warm debate; he had, he said, strenuously advocated peace, and that we should be released, and the terms required by the Ambassadors conceded, before any fresh concessions were demanded. Then, turning round to us, Hang-ki spoke to the following effect,—" Do not mistake; it is not for the sake of yourselves individually I advocate your release; far from it, for, if I thought it would benefit our position, I would advocate your death; but it is because I know your people. I am better acquainted with their powers of destruction than the other Commissioners are. I know they will carry out their threat and destroy Pekin if harm falls on you two; this will bring misery on the people and destruction upon us. No one is allowed to leave the city; my family is here, and I have much property in that part of the town which is the most open to the fire of your shells. I tell you all this, that you may know I have been sincere in my endeavour to save you, not for your own sakes, but for the people's and for my own, but I have failed; now all is lost, the last hope gone.—The Council, which I have just left, have decided to reject the demands of the Allies, call up all the mighty reserves of the Empire, and declare war to the knife; and I have been commissioned to bear to you the decision of the Council, that your execution is to take place this evening." Hang-ki then said that, at his request, two hours were given us, and as we might probably wish to write a few parting words to our friends, he pledged his word to take charge of one letter from each of us, and undertake their delivery to Wade after our death. He then handed to Parkes a locket that contained a miniature photograph of his wife, which had been taken from him the day of our capture, and Hang-ki said that, thinking it would give Parkes pleasure to see it once more before he died, he had taken much pains to recover it for him, and promised to have it delivered with the letters to Wade. We bowed and thanked him, and he left us alone.

As we had been accustomed to look for death at any hour, we felt almost relief that our fate was now decided; we knew we were beyond all human aid; that we had done all we honourably could to warn the Chinese Government of the danger of their conduct; and having failed, we now only hoped we should be able to face the cruel death which was in store for us, bravely together.

Our servants brought us paper, and we wrote what we firmly believed to be our last wishes and feelings in this world. I wrote to my brother, who was staying with the Embassy, and through him sent messages to Lord Elgin, and to those whom I thought would care to be remembered by me at such a time.

Our letters were finished and closed by the time Hang-ki returned; we handed them to him, and he promised to charge himself with their delivery. He was nervous and restless, but Parkes did not allude to our position, but quietly talked on any subject that was mentioned. Messages were brought from time to time to Hang-ki, and he appeared to return verbal answers; at last he gave us back our letters, saying, that our execution was postponed till the morning, until the result of a further communication to Lord Elgin could be known. He said, he had returned to the Council after leaving us, and had urged strongly for this course, which had now received the sanction of Prince Kung. Hang-ki said, "Keep your letters till the morning; you may wish to add to what you have already written." The delay appeared an additional cruelty, for we did not believe, from the temper of the mandarins, that there was the least hope of our ultimate deliverance.

An evening passed as ours was, will bear no description. From our manner the servants and guard could not have learnt that we looked upon our death as certain. We laid down to sleep earlier than usual, being anxious to be awake by daylight.

Saturday, 6th.—In the forenoon Hang-ki called, and his look was so bright that we at once felt he was the bearer of better news. He said he had been up all night with Prince Kung, and that after much anxious consideration the Prince had decided he would intimate to Lord Elgin his acceptance of the terms demanded by the Allies, upon the understanding that no other conditions should be enforced or added to the Treaty or Convention, and that we should communicate this to Lord Elgin, together with a request that no special demand should be made as compensation for the treatment we individually had received. We consented, and Parkes wrote letters to this effect. Hang-ki then took leave of us, and said, if all went well we might hope to be released in a few days. Knowing the uncertain character of the Chinese, we endeavoured not to place too much reliance on Hang-ki's statements; we felt we had passed through an immediate and great peril; it remained to be seen whether it was but a temporary reprieve or permanent safety. It was impossible not to feel hope. We walked for some hours in the courtyard.

This evening, when sitting in our room, Parkes discovered a small piece of paper pasted on the leg of one of the chairs; it had Chinese characters on it, to the effect, that this piece of furniture had been returned into store (naming the department of the

Government), after having been supplied for the use of "the American tribute-bearer, Ward." This was a curious confirmation of the wisdom of Sir F. Bruce's policy in declining to go to Pekin, in 1859, on the conditions accepted by the United States Minister.

Sunday, 7th.—As dawn was breaking I was roused out of a restless sleep by the booming sound of a heavy gun. I sprang up and called out to Parkes, who was lying within a yard or two from me, giving him a push at the same time, "The bombardment has opened at last." Another and another gun followed; by this time we had thrown on our coats, and had gone into the courtyard to hear more distinctly. We found the servants and guard there before us. They said nothing, but eyed us with alarm and curiosity as we walked quietly up and down, without exhibiting by our manner any sign of anxiety. The guns suddenly ceased; the fire had been slow, not so much like the opening of a bombardment as the continued fire after the first burst. For some moments our feelings were very bitter indeed against those mandarins who, we considered, by their obstinate procrastination, had at last brought destruction on their city, and death to us, and to thousands of the unfortunate inhabitants. God knows they had had ample warning of the danger to which their folly had exposed them. We expected each moment the fire would re-open, but as minute followed minute, and at last a full hour elapsed, without hearing another gun, we began again to hope. We cudgelled our brains to think what great event had ever occurred on a 7th of October, the recollection of which was to be kept in men's minds by such an early salute, but we could think of none, so we paced backwards and forwards, feeling sure we should not have long to remain ignorant of what had happened. At about 6.30 we heard the loud shouts which proclaimed the approach of a great man, and at once took our stations at the top of the low flight of steps leading to our room, where we always stood to receive visitors of distinction, conducting them, after many chin-chins, into our apartment, where there ensued a polite struggle as to which of us should occupy the seats of honour, which, however, always ended in the mandarins taking them.

We had scarcely reached our places, when the door leading into the yard was thrown violently open, and Hang-ki hurried in, pushing rudely past us as he went straight into our room, demanding to know the meaning of the guns. Parkes replied, that we looked for that information rather from him; that we had no means of knowing, whereas we presumed he had; but that if we did offer a suggestion, it would be that the Chinese Government, true to its character of procrastination and falsehood, had at last brought upon itself, and the unfortunate inhabitants of Pekin, that punishment of which it had had full warning, a warning it had blindly refused to accept. Hang-ki said, this was no time for such remarks. While he was still speaking, two or three military mandarins entered, and whispered to Hang-ki that the guns had not been shotted. Parkes overheard this; we then concluded it must have been some salute or signal, but thought it better to allow the panic the fear of the attack had evidently caused, to work a little longer, hoping it might induce the Chinese Government to accept at once the conditions required by the Allies. Parkes therefore did not enlighten them, although we were almost convinced that our surmise was correct. Hang-ki now told us for the first time the real position of affairs; he said, the Allied armies were on the north of the city; that immediately the guns had been heard this morning, all the gates were closed and strengthened by sandbags piled against them, so that those inside could not leave the city; that the walls were manned, and great excitement prevailed. That this was true, we knew from the shouts and sounds which occasionally found their way into our room; and Hang-ki added, "Your lives are in imminent danger from the soldiery and populace." He then asked what we would advise. Parkes told him the only advice we could give was what had been already suggested, but which had been treated with contempt; and that the immediate release of all the prisoners was the only means by which the city could be saved from destruction. Hang-ki said, of himself, he was powerless to do this; that it could only be done by an order from Prince Kung; that the Prince was outside the city, and he was uncertain where to look for him, for he now acknowledged that the Allied armies had captured Yuen-Ming-Yuen, the Emperor's summer palace, the night before, where Prince Kung had been residing. However, Hang-ki said he would make one more effort to save Pekin, and that he would at once endeavour to find Prince Kung. He then left, promising to let us know what transpired. The rest of the forenoon passed in much anxiety. About the middle of the day, Hang-ki's servant, who used occasionally to bring messages, called, and after a little hesitation, implored our assistance to save his family. It appeared a curious change, to turn from being the threatened into being the protecting, and Parkes asked how we could assist him; he then gave us full details, so far as he was acquainted with them, of the occurrences of last night. The sudden advance of the Allied armies had taken the Chinese so much by surprise, that both Prince Kung and the Emperor's mother were very nearly captured, the latter only escaping out of the garden adjoining the palace as the troops entered in front. We, I confess, regretted the lady's escape, as her capture would have ensured our safety. He then told us that his wife and children had been at Yuen-Ming-Yuen, that he could hear nothing of their fate, and was in the greatest anxiety; that no one dared to go near the Palace for fear of our soldiers, and he begged that we would give him a pass to go and search for his family, with letters requesting the commanding officers to grant them protection in the event of their lives being in danger. We at once complied with his request, and furnished the letters he required. Parkes then asked as to the state of affairs in Pekin. He replied, everything was in confusion; that there had been daily discussions, the majority of the Council being in favour of our being put to death, and war being carried on with vigour; that this policy had only been hindered by the activity of the minority, at the head of which party was Hang-ki. He told us Hang-ki had had great difficulty in leaving the city this morning; that after he had left us, "great mandarin and officer of state as he is," his servant said, he had not been allowed to pass through the gates, but had been lowered down over the walls in a basket,—a treatment, the old man exclaimed with tears in his eyes, to which no mandarin in his master's position had ever before been subjected. He promised to let us know when Hang-ki returned, and, profuse in his thanks for the letters we had given him, took his leave.

The afternoon and evening appeared interminable. The cries that resounded from time to time in the city, and their occasional near approach, made us expect at any moment an attempt would be made to force our prison. Our guards we heard had been increased to between four and five thousand men.

Monday, 8th.—At daylight we sent to inquire at his house if Hang-ki had yet returned; we received a message that he had come back about four o'clock this morning, much exhausted, but would call about nine. Shortly after that hour he came; he said, he had succeeded in seeing Prince Kung and also Wade; that the latter had said the surrender of one of the gates into the hands of the Allies was a condition the Allied Commanders-in-Chief insisted upon before they would stay further military operations.

This, Hang-ki said, was a demand which could not be complied with; then dismissing the subject, he changed the conversation, and began to discuss a dozen indifferent subjects, amongst others, whether the earth revolved round the sun or vice versâ. He had been joined by a good number of mandarins; all of them quietly drank their tea, and joined in the conversation, — Parkes maintaining his share in it with as much calmness as if our lives, and probably the future fate of China, were not hanging on each moment of valuable time thus slipping away. Not even having the excitement of knowing what was passing, except what Parkes from time to time told me, and yet to appear utterly indifferent, was a great trial of both nerve and temper. At about noon a mandarin called, who had a long whispered conversation with Hang-ki. Hang-ki then returned to his seat, and after drinking a cup of tea, quietly said to Parkes that Prince Kung had decided upon releasing us at once, and that we should be sent, about two o'clock that afternoon, into the Allied camp. Parkes merely bowed in answer, and when he told me, said, "Don't exhibit any pleasure or feeling." I suggested that as the discussion about the sun and earth must be by this time nearly exhausted, he should ask their opinion as to whether the moon rotates on her own axis, which I believed was considered still a doubtful point in Europe. Without saying one word respecting our release, Parkes quietly began on this subject and continued until Hang-ki's patience was exhausted, when he exclaimed: "You appear to be alike indifferent as to whether you are to die or live." Parkes replied: "Not at all; but we have now had considerable experience of the vacillation and deceit of the Chinese Government, and therefore until our release becomes an accomplished fact, we venture to doubt it." Hang-ki had now risen and was walking up and down the room; he suddenly went up to Parkes, and leaning forward, whispered in his ear: "There are many difficulties to be overcome; you cannot leave before two o'clock, but you cannot be more anxious to hurry forward the arrangements than I am. If we ever meet after to-day, remind me, and I will tell you my reasons."

We were told six other prisoners would be released at the same time, but we could not ascertain who they were. Our servants now busied themselves and packed up our very few possessions; and Hang-ki presented a cloth cloak to each of us. We waited anxiously for two o'clock;—it came at last. Hang-ki, who for the previous hour had been passing backwards and forwards, then came and led us by the hand into an outer court, where we found three or four covered carts,—the curtains round them were closed and prevented our seeing who were inside. Parkes and I got into the one prepared for us; the curtain was then drawn, and we were told to be careful not to show ourselves. Some little time was occupied, apparently in forming the escort; when all was in readiness, the gate leading into the street was thrown open. A dense crowd had assembled outside; the escort cleared a way for the carts, and men went in front with whips to keep the people back. It is impossible to describe our feelings—our hopes were raised—and yet we felt how much still lay between us and safety.

The large body of troops, not under three thousand men, required to clear the way, alone showed the resistance it was anticipated our release would meet with from the people. A fine large mule drew our cart, which was comfortably fitted with pillows and cushions.

We soon saw we were going towards the most northern of the western gates of the city, the high towers of which we could see rising in front of us. We had been told that Hang-ki had been lowered from the walls, because the soldiers would not open the gates even to admit of his passing out to meet Prince Kung, and therefore we felt very apprehensive that they might refuse to allow us to pass. It seemed as if we should never reach the gate; at last we had a good view of the heavy massive doors, which with a sickening feeling we saw were closed, but when within thirty yards they were thrown open, and we heard the heavy bang of their being shut behind us with a sensation of intense relief. The outer gate was opened and closed in the same manner, and we found ourselves once more outside the walls of Pekin and in the open country.

We had not moved forward many yards when the mule-driver stopped and asked where he was to go to. We then found for the first time that our escort had left us, and that there were only the carts and the mule drivers. Parkes asked where the Allied armies were, and told the man to drive us in that direction; but as the man professed complete ignorance, Parkes told him to follow a road that ran to the north under the city walls. As we went along, Parkes entered into conversation with him, and after a little while got him to speak about his wife and family, and it ended by Parkes promising to engage the whole of them at a rate of wages which to the muleteer appeared untold wealth. His sympathies having been thus enlisted in our favour, he said he thought he could take us somewhere near to our army, but advised us to keep well concealed in the cart, as he thought it probable, if seen, they might fire at us from the walls; and on looking through the curtain, we saw that they were manned by matchlockmen.

When we arrived at the N.W. angle of the wall, we found the road turned sharp to the east, running along the north face; we decided on following this, and after travelling about two miles we came to the An-ting gate, which was the one the Commanders-in-Chief demanded should be surrendered to the Allies. It was, however, very evident, from the flags and soldiers on the walls, that it was still in the possession of the Chinese. Opposite to this gate a road branched off to the northward, and as our mule-driver said he thought it would lead in the direction of our army, Parkes told him to follow it. After proceeding along it about half a mile, the road passed through a straggling collection of houses; in about the centre of this village (if village it could be called) was a large temple, surrounded by the usual number of enclosed courts. Several mandarins, with their servants, were waiting in front of the gate; they stopped the carts, and begged us to alight to take some refreshments before going into camp; they said Hang-ki was coming, but as he had not mentioned to us his intention of doing so, we did not believe the statement, and it made us suspicious. We told the mandarins that we did not want food, but wished to reach our army; they however pressed it so much, we were induced to accompany them through two or three courtyards, when, finding nothing but a small table scantily provided with fruit, I began to fear treachery, and begged Parkes to return to the road. As he shared this opinion, we insisted on going back; the mandarins entreated us to stay, but we pushed them aside and got back to the carts. As yet we did not know who were inside of them; in the first we found Nal-Sing, the old Sikh; when he saw us he jumped out and knelt down, embracing our legs in his great joy; in the other carts, which we half thought might contain some of our comrades, we found five French, two of them the soldiers who had accompanied us to Pekin, two other soldiers, and Count D'Escayrac de Lauture, who, we learnt afterwards, had been captured the same day as ourselves. Parkes and I had determined that sooner than consent to recapture, we would make a run and the best fight of it we could, as death was preferable to the life we had been living. I told our determination to the others, and they all declared they would do the same. By this time they had got out of the carts, and in spite of the entreaties of the mandarins, we walked on; we had scarcely gone a quarter of a mile, when we saw a small crowd, apparently of villagers, with baskets of vegetables, and, to our intense joy, a red-coat. The pleasure of that sight, and the feeling of safety and sense of relief it imparted, it is impossible to describe. We hurried forward; the sentry observing our approach, called to the corporal of the outlying picket; he came forward, and we all shook hands most heartily together. The corporal sent word of our arrival to the inlying picket, where we met Major James, who led us to head-quarters. As we passed across the large plain on which our army was encamped, men came running from all directions to give us a hearty welcome; and thus led in triumph we reached the temple Lord Elgin and Sir Hope Grant occupied, where we received the most affectionate reception from all our friends.

We now learnt for the first time that we were the only ones of our party who had as yet escaped; and deeply grateful did we feel to that merciful Providence which had watched over our safety through so many dangers. Perhaps only those who have passed through similar scenes and anxieties can fully realise the intense relief we now experienced in both mind and body.

Although I did not become acquainted with the following circumstances, subsequently narrated by Hang-ki, for several months after the period of our release, I may perhaps relate them here, as they explain the reason of his great anxiety to get us out of Pekin before two o'clock, and as they make our escape more miraculous than at the time it even appeared to ourselves.

Several months passed before Parkes had any opportunity of asking Hang-ki for the explanation he had promised; indeed, he had forgotten all about it until reminded by Hang-ki. Hang-ki told him that the Emperor, who had retired to Jehol, in Manchooria, had been surrounded by the leaders of the anti-progressive party, who were in favour of a war policy, and that they constantly urged the Emperor to order the execution of the prisoners, as they considered, if this were done, it would commit men of all parties, and be the means of obliging them to combine, for their common safety, to resist the Allied armies; that two or three times this policy was on the point of being carried out, but the active resistance offered to it by the leaders of the minority had been successful in procuring delay. Hang-ki had spies at Jehol, who kept him informed daily of all that passed. On the morning of the 8th,—the day we were released,—one of his messengers arrived with the intelligence that the Emperor had at last consented to the representations of the war party, and had signed the order for the immediate execution of the prisoners,—Parkes and myself being specially mentioned by name; and that the Government courier was on his way, and could only be a few hours behind him. Hang-ki having thus timely notice, succeeded in persuading Prince Kung to order our release; the sudden advance of the armies and capture of Yuen-Ming-Yuen having greatly alarmed him, and made him more willing to listen to Hang-ki's statements as to the power of the Allies to inflict a severe punishment on Pekin in retribution for any injury done to us. From the information he had received, Hang-ki expected the Government courier would arrive between two and three o'clock, and therefore hurried forward the preparations for our release; and, he added, "If your deliverance had been only delayed a quarter of an hour, even Prince Kung's influence could not have saved you, as the Emperor's order for the immediate execution of yourself and Loch, without any further delay, arrived within fifteen minutes of your having passed through the gates."

We had indeed cause to be most humbly grateful for our merciful preservation.

CHAPTER XIII.

PROCEEDINGS OF THE ALLIED ARMIES FROM THE 18TH SEPTEMBER,—THE DAY OF OUR CAPTURE, TO THE 8TH OF OCTOBER,—THE DAY OF OUR RELEASE.

I WILL briefly relate the operations of the Allied armies from the time I left Sir Hope Grant on the morning of the 18th of September, after communicating to him the position of affairs, up to the day of our release, the 8th of October.

It will be remembered that Colonel Walker and his party remained on the bund which was on the bank of the stream behind which the Chinese army were formed in line of battle, concealed from the view of the Allied armies by the embankment, and by the trees and tall millet which was still standing, and of which the Chinese had availed themselves in the selection of their position.

For some time after Parkes had returned to Tung-chow, and I had passed the Chinese outposts to communicate with Sir Hope Grant, Colonel Walker and his party remained unmolested; he moved backwards and forwards along the top of the embankment, within a few yards of the Chinese infantry. As time passed, and reinforcements kept arriving, the Chinese began to be insolent in their manner; but knowing how much the safety of the party in Tung-chow depended on his being able to ward off any open hostilities till sufficient time had elapsed to enable it to escape, he maintained his anxious and difficult position. Upwards of an hour had passed, when the Chinese, now careless for further concealment as their troops were nearly all in position, and possibly having acquired confidence from the quiet indifference with which their insults had been received, resorted to personal violence: a few of them climbed on to the bank, and while pretending to speak civilly, attempted to jerk Colonel Walker's sword out of the scabbard.

A vast grassy plain extended between Colonel Walker's party and the Allied armies, which were only about three-quarters of a mile distant, with only a few Tartar cavalry vedettes between. Seeing matters were now assuming a serious aspect, Colonel Walker warned his men to be ready to gallop across the intervening space. This was not likely to be attended with much danger, as the Chinese, unprepared for a sudden movement of this kind, would only be able to fire a random volley after them. Anxious, however, to remain as long as a proper consideration for the safety of his party justified it, he still endeavoured to delay the moment, and avoid a quarrel by moving from place to place. It was from this cause that I missed seeing him when I passed through the Chinese army with Brabazon on my return to Tung-chow.

At last, I have been given to understand, an attempt was made either to seize his rein or sword, but he gave the word for the party to gallop for their lives. The movement was so quick, that they had gained some distance before an ineffectual volley was fired, and they reached the Allied armies in a few minutes, without loss. Mr. Thompson, of the Commissariat department, was the only one hurt; he received a lance wound from one of the vedettes as he passed.

The volley fired after Colonel Walker and his party was the signal for the Chinese to open with upwards of seventy guns, which it was said they had in position; their fire was immediately answered by the Allies, and it was the first shell that was fired, which we saw bursting in the air, as we cleared the town of Chang-kia-wan. Another fifteen minutes and in all probability we should have been safe.

Sir Hope Grant, with great skill, had succeeded for upwards of an hour and a half in delaying any offensive movement; and Colonel Walker, with a patience and courage deserving of great praise, remained in a position which required much calmness and judgment, and held this post of some peril as long as he considered it tenable.

Very shortly after the battle commenced, a rapid advance of the Allies forced the Chinese to retire. The cavalry had many opportunities, of which they did not fail to take advantage, of distinguishing themselves.

The enemy was said to have at least twenty thousand cavalry in the field. The Chinese army were driven back on Tung-chow; in the pursuit, some of our troops—infantry as well as cavalry—followed the enemy beyond that city round its western wall, but rejoined the army before dark where it had halted near Chang-kia-wan. The Chinese suffered a severe defeat, and lost many guns; their loss in killed and wounded was also considerable; that of the Allies was comparatively trifling.

Mr. Wade, with a flag of truce, advanced to one of the gates of Tung-chow, and endeavoured to ascertain the fate of the prisoners: he ran great personal risk in the attempt, but throughout this day, and on many subsequent occasions, he embraced every opportunity that offered, regardless of danger to himself, to re-open personal communication with the Chinese officials with a view of bringing about a settlement of the existing differences, and to secure our safety; and his efforts were at last rewarded with success.

The army remained halted near Tung-chow until the 21st, when having received supplies, the Allied Commanders-in-Chief again advanced. The Chinese now occupied the position which had been held by Juilin on the 18th, when we were taken to his camp; it was about three miles beyond Tung-chow, and covered the road to Pekin. Pah-li-chiao bridge was also held, which indeed was the key of the Chinese position. The French directed their attack on this point, while the English operated on the left, doubling up the right of the Chinese army. The Chinese held their position with great bravery, but were driven from it by the superior fire of the Allied artillery and rifles. The French suffered severely at their attack on the bridge; the loss of the English was small. The officer who commanded the Chinese division of the army opposed to the French was twice wounded during the attack, and it has been subsequently stated that Brabazon and Abbé de Luc, being at the time in his camp, he, out of revenge, had them beheaded from the parapet of the bridge. The evidence in support of this statement will be related hereafter.

The Chinese after this defeat retreated to Pekin, and occupied a position to the east and north-east of the city. The Allies only advanced a few miles beyond Tung-chow, along the road leading to Pekin, and there halted to await supplies and reinforcements from Tien-tsin; and as it was now necessary to prepare for all eventualities, the Commanders-in-Chief considered it essential to bring up the siege guns before any further forward movement was attempted.

During this period of comparative inaction the Ambassadors communicated by letter with the Chinese authorities, warning them that if any harm befell the prisoners a severe punishment would be exacted. The Imperial Government endeavoured to prevent the further advance of the armies, by threatening that an onward move would be the signal for the prisoners' execution. Lord Elgin, however, saw from the first that their only chance of safety depended on the Allied armies carrying out with vigour those measures which, whether the prisoners' lives did or did not depend on the result, it was the duty of the Allies to adopt; and therefore he informed the Chinese authorities that he would sign no Convention with the Imperial Commissioners except within the walls of Pekin, and that if the prisoners were put to death he would destroy that city. The stronger the threats of the Chinese, the more determined Lord Elgin's language became. From the first the Chinese made the great mistake of supposing they could deter Lord Elgin from following the line of policy which in his opinion was the most likely, by humbling the war party, to bring about a speedy termination of the war,—by a threat which he would most properly have disregarded even if he had been assured beyond all doubt that it would lead to the result threatened. But as it was, he considered the only chance of saving the lives of the prisoners was the adoption of that policy which he deemed it advisable for Imperial interests to follow; and the result showed how correctly he had judged the Chinese character.

Referring to somewhat similar incidents of a more recent period, I cannot help thinking that Lord Napier's conduct with reference to the release of the prisoners in Abyssinia was partly guided by the recollection of what had occurred at the time of which I speak, in China; as at that time Sir Robert Napier commanded a division of the army, and was fully acquainted with Lord Elgin's views and opinions on these points.

The Allied Commanders-in-Chief required several days to complete their most necessary arrangements, as it was of paramount importance—both on account of the approach of winter, and as it was in the power of the Chinese, had they possessed a General competent of handling the very large cavalry force they possessed (estimated at the lowest at thirty thousand), to have greatly retarded if not entirely checked the advance of the Allies by cutting off their extended line of communication with their base of operations at Tien-tsin and Taku,—to establish at Tung-chow, which city had surrendered to the Allies, large depots of supplies to provide against this danger, and secure a greater freedom of action.

By the beginning of October the army was again ready to advance. The communications that had passed with the Chinese authorities had led to no result, and probably the compelled inactivity of the army, with the true reasons for which they were of course unacquainted, made them as unyielding and as full of evasion as they had been previous to their recent defeats.

On the east and south of Pekin large suburbs extend several miles beyond the walls, which cannot therefore be easily approached, but on the north-east, north, and north-west sides, the country is quite open to the base of the walls. The country in this direction is pretty free from enclosures; an occasional temple surrounded by the usual extensive courtyards, with a few scattered houses, and very small villages at long distances apart, being all that could obstruct the approach of a large force.

On the 6th of October the Allies moved round the north-east angle of the wall, so as to gain this open plain,—keeping at some little distance from the city. There was no appearance of any large body of the enemy, and only a few shots were exchanged between the advance guard and a few Chinese vedettes. The French were on the right of the line, and during the march became separated from the English; the cavalry also, under Brigadier Pattle, had pushed forward, and towards night found themselves in roads bounded by high walls, which seemed to be enclosures to large buildings. Owing, however, to the darkness, and the Chinese having fled, they could obtain no accurate information as to their position.

Sir Hope Grant became very anxious as night came on, and he was still ignorant of the position both of the French army and of the cavalry; and ordered the artillery to fire a few blank rounds to acquaint General de Montauban and Brigadier Pattle with the whereabouts of the English army. Lord Elgin hearing of this, begged the General to defer firing any guns until the morning, as it was impossible to judge the effect which the alarm it was sure to cause in Pekin might have on the Chinese, and the extent to which it might endanger the lives of the prisoners. Sir Hope Grant at once consented to defer firing the signal until the morning, when the Chinese would perceive the guns were not directed against the town. Most fortunate was Lord Elgin's thoughtful consideration, for if the General had carried out his original intention, the result, judging from the excitement the guns created, as I have already related, when they were fired even in daylight, would probably have proved fatal to us.

The following morning it was ascertained that the cavalry had passed the night close to the Emperor's summer palace of Yuen-Ming-Yuen; the French had also been there, and had occupied several of the buildings. On receiving this intelligence, prize officers and a detachment were, I believe, at once despatched to look after the English interests. During the 7th and 8th the army occupied a position in front of the north wall, concentrating their strength principally opposite the An-ting gate.

Lord Elgin and Sir Hope Grant took up their quarters with their respective staffs in a very fine and large temple; the numerous yards and buildings affording good accommodation to the servants, guards, horses, &c. It was about a mile and a half to two miles from Pekin.

Frequent communications now passed between Prince Kung and Lord Elgin, the latter insisting on a strict compliance with all his demands, including the surrender of a gate of the city, and the release of the prisoners. Although the result proved the contrary, much doubt existed, even presuming his opinion was favourable to a conciliatory policy, whether Prince Kung had really the power of carrying out any arrangement he might conclude. However, Lord Elgin's strong, consistent and determined policy won the day;—it gained Prince Kung, and Hang-ki by his management and energy overcame the other difficulties, and by the release of all the surviving prisoners negotiations were renewed with a fair prospect of their being ultimately brought to a satisfactory conclusion.

CHAPTER XIV.

SURRENDER OF THE BODIES OF MESSRS. DE NORMANN, ANDERSON, BOWLBY, PHIPPS, AND THOSE OF NINE SIKHS, TOGETHER WITH THE RETURN OF TEN SIKHS AND THREE FRENCH SOLDIERS, — SURVIVORS. — NEGOTIATIONS.

Tuesday, the 9th.—I think my feelings on waking this morning were the most agreeable I ever experienced—the weight on the mind with which each day, for the last three weeks, I had awoke, was replaced by a sense of rest and repose; to interfere with which, no sufficient time had as yet elapsed for any lesser trouble to exaggerate itself into such importance as to occupy the place in the mind which had been filled by the trouble it had just discarded.

We learnt that the An-ting gate was not yet surrendered, and a communication received from Prince Kung raised fresh difficulties to a compliance with this condition. The Allied Commanders-in-Chief therefore gave the Chinese authorities till noon of the 13th to decide, informing them if they failed to surrender the gate by that date hostilities would be re-commenced.

In the meantime, the Artillery and Engineers have taken possession of a temple within a short distance of the city wall, a little to the eastward of the An-ting gate; and under cover of the wall of the courtyard nearest to the town are getting the siege guns and mortars into position.

Wednesday, the 10*th.*—Engaged all day drawing up an official report addressed to Lord Elgin, detailing the circumstances that preceded and led to the capture of the prisoners, together with a statement as far as my knowledge extends of their subsequent treatment. The mail left this afternoon for England.

Thursday, the 11*th.*—Lord Elgin decided to dispatch H.M.S. "Furious" to Shanghai for Sir Frederick Bruce. My brother takes this opportunity of returning homewards, and will start early to-morrow with Captain Jones, R.N., for Tien-tsin.

The Chinese have promised that some of the surviving prisoners shall be sent into camp to-morrow; as yet we have been unable to ascertain how many are still living.

Friday, the 12*th.* — Immediately after breakfast the party returning to Shanghai started on their ride to Tien-tsin.

In the afternoon we went to meet the prisoners; there were eight Sikhs and three French soldiers, four of the Sikhs had been with Anderson and De Normann, the others had been with Phipps of the King's Dragoon Guards, and some French officers who had been captured about the same time as ourselves; all of whom had died. The French soldiers who were released appear to have been by themselves, for they could give no information of any kind. The wrists of the Sikhs showed the severity with which they had been bound. I will relate later more of the particulars given by these poor fellows.

Saturday, 13*th.*—The batteries were completed last night, and every preparation made for opening fire at noon to-day, but a message came, saying the An-ting gate would be surrendered. It was accordingly taken possession of by the 97th Regiment, 8th Punjabs, and Desborough's Battery.

The gate, which opens direct into the city, is protected by a wall of great thickness, extending in a semicircular form, the convex side being towards the country, and thus protects the gate itself from any direct attack. The enclosure which this wall forms is entered by a gate opening at right angles to the city wall, and near to where it is joined by the easternmost arm of the encircling wall. The main wall of the city is about sixty feet in height, the thickness at the top about fifty. The breadth at the base cannot be less than seventy to eighty feet; the height of the inner part of the wall above the city is in places from forty to fifty feet. There is a large building above the gate, which is used partly as a barrack and store. In some of the embrasures in this upper building wooden guns are mounted. The thickness of the semicircular wall is not so great as the main one, although very considerable. I doubt whether if all our siege guns had fired at it for a week, they could have effected any practicable breach in a work of such solid construction.

From information we received to-day we fear there is no hope of Bowlby and Brabazon being alive.

Sunday, 14th.—We had Church service in a large room in the temple.

In the afternoon two more Sikhs were brought in by the Chinese, they were the last of the survivors; they had been with poor Bowlby, and present when he died, which was about the fifth day after our capture.

This evening the bodies of De Normann, Anderson, and two Sikhs were brought in. It was dark when they arrived; by torchlight we examined them,—the Chinese had put quicklime into the coffins in which the bodies had been placed, and it was impossible to recognise them by their features.—Poor De Normann we knew by his boots and a piece of leather coat he always wore, some of his hair and beard also remained,—Anderson we also recognised by his clothes. Both were men of great promise, and would doubtless have risen to honour and distinction in their respective professions.

The sight of these bodies, victims to the

treacherous policy of the Chinese government, excited general indignation. To Parkes and myself it was a most bitter grief that after sharing with us the pains and trials of captivity they had not lived to share with us the blessings of release. Before our own escape we had almost argued ourselves into the belief, from Hang-ki avoiding all mention with reference to their fate, that they had escaped.

The bodies of Bowlby and Phipp, and those of the remaining Sikhs, were brought in on the 16th. Quicklime had destroyed their features but we recognised them by their clothes, and Bowlby, poor fellow, we also knew from the peculiar formation of his head and brow and by a peculiarity in one of his feet. Strangely enough, about six weeks earlier he had related to us his having gone to Wales to the spot where the " Royal Charter" had been wrecked, to search amongst the bodies of those washed on shore for that of a brother who had been lost, and after several days he had recognised one—the features of which were defaced from the length of time the body had been in the sea—to be that of his brother by a peculiar formation in his foot, caused, I think he said, by a broken bone. It was a singular coincidence that almost the only way by which his own body was identified within so short a time of his telling this story was by a similar peculiarity in one of his feet. The Chinese stated that Brabazon and Abbé de Luc were beheaded on the 21st ultimo at Pah-li-chiao.

The bodies which had been delivered, so clearly demonstrated the cruelties which had been inflicted, that Lord Elgin at once notified to Prince Kung that he was too horrified by what had occurred to hold further communication with a government guilty of such deeds of treachery and bloodshed, until by some great punishment inflicted upon the Emperor and the governing classes he had made apparent to the whole Empire and the world, the detestation with which the Allies viewed such conduct.

Wednesday, the 17th, was the day arranged for the burial of those whose bodies had been surrendered. The place selected was the Russian Cemetery, which is about a mile from the north-east angle of the city wall; officers and men from every regiment attended, the coffins were conveyed on gun-carriages; General de Montauban and many French officers were present. The procession moved slowly across the plain. Lord Elgin and Sir Hope Grant were the chief mourners, Parkes and myself next.

A long trench had been dug, and the coffins were placed side by side, and when at the close of the service the earth was thrown in, the unusual sight was witnessed of Protestant, Roman Catholic, and Greek Church priests meeting in Christian charity and praying together over one grave.

The following accounts of the deaths of De Normann and the other prisoners were related by duffadar Jawalla Sing, sowar Bughel Sing, and sowar Khan Sing, all of Fane's Horse:—

Evidence of Jawalla Sing, duffadar, 1st troop Fane's Horse:—

When Messrs. Parkes and Loch left our party for the purpose of seeing San-ko-lin-sin, there were Mr. Bowlby, Lieut. Anderson, Capt. Brabazon, Mr. De Normann, one man King's Dragoon Guards, one man 1st Sikh Cavalry, and our own party of seventeen men. We stood waiting for half an hour, when Mr. Anderson asked to be taken where the other gentlemen were gone. He was told to remain till they came back. After another half hour, the army assembled in large numbers and surrounded us, told us to get off our horses, and leading them to come with them; then the whole army, as Lieut. Anderson remarked, about ten thousand men, took us back to Tung-chow, and made us rest for a quarter of an hour, and give up our arms. They then made us remount, and paraded us through the army, and then took us on the road to Pekin, and rested that night in a joss house. In the morning they again mounted us on our horses and took us to Pekin; in Pekin they made us dismount and fed us; they then took us through the city to a place about two miles beyond it, there they made us dismount and gave us tents,—the English officers and natives separate. Then they took us away one by one and bound us, lying on the stomach with hands and feet tied behind the back;—they kept us there in this position for three days, they gave us food three times, and that only a mouthful at a time; they then threw us, bound as we were, into carts, and took us, as I think, about twenty coss—the mules were trotting and galloping all night. We arrived in the morning at a Fort Showja (I think it was called), and were there put into prison, confined in cages and loaded with chains. At that time we were seven in all,—Anderson, De Normann, one duffadar, and four sowars. I know nothing of the others, they were taken further on. We were kept in this place three days, so tightly bound we couldn't move; the sowars bound with one cord, the others with two. At the first place we got nothing to eat; after that they gave us a little as before. After the first day, at the same place (outside the Emperor's palace, about three miles from Pekin), Lieut. Anderson became delirious, and remained so, with a few lucid intervals, until his death, which occurred on the ninth day of his imprisonment.—Before his death his nails and fingers burst from the tightness of the cords, and mortification set in, and the bones of the wrist were exposed,—whilst he was alive, worms were generated in his wounds, and ate into, and crawled over his body. They left the body there three days, and then took it away; five days after this a sowar named Ramden died in the same state,—his body was taken away immediately. Three days after this, Mr. De Normann died. On the evening of Lieut. Anderson's decease the cords were taken off our hands, and from that time we were better fed; our feet were unbound two days after this, and kept so until our release yesterday evening. When Lieut. Anderson and our comrades called on us to help by biting his cords the Chinamen kicked us away.

When we arrived at the joss house between Tung-chow and Pekin, Captain Brabazon and the Frenchman went back, and Lieut. Anderson told us they were going to the Commanders-in-Chief to give information and obtain our release.

Deposition of Bughel Sing, sowar, 1st troop Fane's Horse; and also of sowar Khan Sing, of the same regiment.

The first day we stopped at a joss house on the side of the road to Pekin; we tied our horses up, and went inside. The Chinese then took them away, but brought them back in the morning, and we again mounted. Here two gentlemen left us; we went through Pekin to the other side, and pulled up at a serai; here one of the Chinamen went to ask if we should dismount, and on his return we were taken to some tents. This place had barracks inside, and we went through a large doorway. We had been there half an hour when we were ordered out one by one to wash our hands and faces. They took out the gentlemen first, threw them down, and fastened their hands behind them. They then made us kneel down in the middle of the yard, tied our hands and feet behind, and threw us over on our backs. From this position, if we attempted to rest on our right or left side, they kicked and beat us. We remained in this position all night, during which time they poured water on our bonds to tighten them. Mr. De Normann spoke to one of the Chinese officers during the night, and told him that we came to treat and not to fight, and they then gave us a little water and rice. The Hindoos would not eat it until Mr. Anderson persuaded them to do so, when some of them did. The next day a white button mandarin came to see us. He had many orderlies with him, and he took down in writing some answers to questions put by him to Mr. De Normann. About two hours after he was gone we were loaded with irons; got nothing more to eat or drink for three days; Mr. Anderson's hands were swollen to three times their proper size, and as black as ink; the whole weight of his body—chains and all—was thrown on his hands, they looked ready to burst. As long as he was sensible he encouraged us, and rebuked us for calling out; when he became insensible he constantly called out Major Fane, Maclean, and others; he became delirious when the chains were put on. On the afternoon of the third day from this, they took four of us away in carts; travelled all that night, gave us no food or water, and beat us when we asked for any. Mr. Bowlby's hands were not so much swollen; he spoke no Hindostanee, and so we could not understand him; at 10 a.m. next day we arrived at a fort, with a few buildings near it, there was no town. Another cart was with us containing duffadar Mahomed Bux, a French officer, very tall and stout, with a brown beard, and a dragoon named Pisa (Phipps). We were taken into the fort, and for three days were out in the open air in the cold. They then pulled us into an old kitchen and kept us there eight days; they never allowed us to stir for three or four days. Mr. Bowlby died the second day after we arrived; he died from maggots forming in his wrists; he was dressed in a kind of grey check. His body remained there nearly three days, and the next day it was tied to a crossbeam and thrown over the wall to be eaten by dogs and pigs. The next day the Frenchman died; he was wounded slightly on the head and hand, apparently by a sword. Maggots got into his ears, nose, and mouth, and he became insensible. He had on a black coat, red trousers with black stripe;—(Deponent does not give a clear account of dress)—he was tall as Major Probin, but stouter. Two days after this Jawalla Sing (first Sikh) died; his hands burst from his rope wounds, maggots got into them, and he died. Four days afterwards, Phipps, King's Dragoon Guards, died; for ten days he encouraged us in every way he could, but one day his hands became swollen like Mr. Anderson's, and maggots were generated the next,—one maggot increased a thousand-fold in a day. Mahomed Bux, duffadar, died ten days ago; he remained very well till then, and abused the Chinese for bringing him pig to eat. Maggots formed on him four days before his death, and his hands were completely eaten away. I should have died had not my chains been taken off.

The Chinaman who brought us here was very kind, he dressed our wounds and gave us what we wanted; when he was absent we got nothing.

The deponent has Mr. Bowlby's stockings.

It now remains only to relate what information we obtained respecting the death of Brabazon and Abbé de Luc. All the Chinese who were not Government officials agreed in asserting they had been beheaded; for the reason, and on the day already stated.

The Chinese authorities denied that they had been put to death, saying they had died like the others from natural causes; they, however, failed to produce their bodies, which was an argument in favour of the statement of their having been beheaded.

The Russian Mission, which had good sources of intelligence, was of opinion the General commanding the division of the Chinese army at Pah-li-chiao bridge had ordered their execution. This has been since confirmed.

Some months later, a spot was pointed out by some Chinese as the place where the bodies had been buried. On search being made, besides bones, a piece of cloth with a red stripe and a small piece of silk were found in the grave. They were sent to England, and the former was declared to be a part of an artillery officer's trousers, while the latter was supposed to be a part of a French ecclesiastic's dress.

No skulls were found in the grave.

CHAPTER XV.

YUEN-MING-YUEN.—A SECOND VISIT TO PEKIN.

AFTER anxious deliberation, Lord Elgin decided to request the Commander-in-Chief to take the requisite steps for the destruction of the Emperor's palace of Yuen-Ming-Yuen. He considered it necessary to mark in a manner that could not soon be forgotten the punishment awarded for an act of treachery so gross as that which had characterised the Emperor's policy, and that had resulted in the murder of so many officers and men. The implication of the Emperor and the Chinese Government in the treatment of the prisoners was proved by De Normann and the others having been taken in the first instance to Yuen-Ming-Yuen, and that there had commenced the ill-usage which resulted in their deaths. Several articles of their clothing were found in the rooms adjoining the Hall of Audience, and nearly all our horses and saddles were recovered from the Royal stables. But while Lord Elgin was desirous of making the punishment to be inflicted apparent to the whole Chinese Empire, and one which could not be glossed over or concealed, it was his anxious wish to make it fall only on the Emperor who had been acquainted with, and was responsible for the commission of the crime.

It may be urged that it was a ruthless act to destroy so much that was rare, beautiful, and valuable; but wonderful as was the extent of the palace, or, more correctly speaking, palaces and gardens,—for there were, it was estimated, upwards of two hundred buildings, and the grounds covered an area of eight by ten miles in extent,—still there was no utter annihilation of works of art or learning; for on good authority it was stated, that nothing unique either in the shape of books or manuscripts was kept at Yuen-Ming-Yuen, and in the subsequent search for both, previous to the burning, very few were found, and certainly none of any exclusive rarity.

Against the natural repugnance which must

always exist in the mind of every educated person to the destruction of the beautiful, must be brought the consideration of the position in which the Allies were placed. Winter was rapidly approaching; the Commanders-in-Chief had already informed the Ambassadors that by an early date the armies would have to retire; the treacherous conduct of which the Government had been guilty was still fresh in the minds of all, Chinese and Europeans alike, and it was felt that if it was allowed to pass without some signal example being made, it would encourage the belief that similar acts could be perpetrated with impunity, and the position of the members of the future resident Embassy in Pekin might be thus endangered if the Imperial Government were not made aware that punishment would surely follow any act of treachery.

It was also felt that no money indemnity could compensate for the insult inflicted; and, moreover, if an indemnity had been enforced, that it would have fallen on the people and not on the Emperor or mandarin classes. It was also desirable in consequence of the early withdrawal of the armies, rendered necessary by the advance of winter, to mark in some way which would place it beyond all dispute, that the Allies had occupied Pekin as conquerors, otherwise the Imperial Government would be apt to deny the fact, and assert that the Allies had been forced to retire by the Imperial army.

To prevent any misconstruction being placed on his motives, and to prove to the Chinese that the Allies did not war with the people, but only with those whose bad faith had already caused so much suffering and bloodshed, Lord Elgin addressed a communication to Prince Kung acquainting him with his decision; and likewise published a proclamation in Chinese, copies of which were affixed on all the buildings and walls in the neighbourhood of the Allied camps and Yuen-Ming-Yuen, to the effect, "That no individual, however exalted, could escape from the responsibility and punishment which must always follow the commission of acts of falsehood and deceit; that Yuen-Ming-Yuen would be burnt on the 18th, as a punishment inflicted on the Emperor for the violation of his word, and the act of treachery to a flag of truce; that as the people were not concerned in these acts no harm would befal them, but the Imperial Government alone would be held responsible."

On the morning of Thursday the 18th, Sir John Mitchell moved with his division to Yuen-Ming-Yuen. The buildings in themselves possessed but little architectural beauty; they were nearly all isolated from each other, being connected by gardens, courts, and terraces. The most striking amongst them were those near the Hall of Audience. The largest of these were connected by courtyards, passing through which were entered spacious reception rooms that opened into gardens of considerable extent, which lead down to a marble terrace stretching along the shores of a lake some three miles in length. Bordering the terrace for a mile or a mile and a half, and opening on to it, were other gardens and buildings,—these were summer houses, and the residences where the Emperor lodged his most distinguished guests. The balustrade, like the terrace, was of white marble, and in places curiously carved. On this stood at intervals of some twenty or thirty yards, beautiful blue inlaid enamel vases with imitation flowers, made of the blood, cornelian, jade, and other valuable stones. The houses were built for hot rather than cold weather, as was apparent from the size of the doors and windows.

There were magnificent bronzes in different parts of the gardens, larger than life, of lions and other animals, but there was one of exceptional beauty of a cow lying down, the workmanship and design of which were very fine. Fortunately all these bronzes were too far from any of the buildings to be injured by fire; indeed, only portions of the buildings themselves were burnt, and although the destruction, from the volumes of smoke, appeared immense, still a great portion escaped, as well as nearly all the valuable enamels, of which there were large quantities in some of the houses.

The money found in the Treasury was of no great amount; it was taken possession of by the prize agents for distribution amongst the troops; and all officers and men who had taken any property previous to the 18th from Yuen-Ming-Yuen, had to hand it over to officers appointed to receive the same; it was all subsequently sold at public auction, the proceeds going to the general fund for distribution to the army. Sir Hope Grant ordered the prize-money to be divided amongst the officers and men at once, thus saving delay, and the necessity for provision being made by the Military Train for the conveyance of the treasure to Taku.

During the whole of Friday the 19th, Yuen-Ming-Yuen was still burning; the clouds of smoke, driven by the wind, hung like a vast black pall over Pekin.

On the morning of Saturday the 20th, Lord Elgin received Prince Kung's absolute submission to all the demands of the Allies, and the Prince requested that an early day should be named for the signature of the Convention and exchange of the Ratifications of the Treaty of Tien-tsin.

Sunday, the 21st.—As it was necessary to select a suitable building within Pekin where the ceremony of the exchange of the Ratifications could take place, the Chinese authorities had been informed that this forenoon a party would be ready to visit, in company with Commissioners appointed by them, the various places they might suggest for this purpose, and also to look at some of the palaces that could be prepared at once for the residence of Lord Elgin and the Embassy.

At about eleven o' clock, Parkes and I, having been deputed by Lord Elgin for this duty, accompanied by Colonel Ross of the Quarter-Master-General's Department, and an escort of fifty men of the King's Dragoon Guards and a few Sikh Irregular Cavalry, entered the An-ting gate, and passed along the north of the city for about a mile, when we turned to the south by the west wall, which we followed until we reached the south Chinese wall, that separates the Tartar from the Chinese city. When we got some little distance from the north wall, we found the streets full of people busy in their usual occupations. Our appearance caused considerable curiosity and excitement, although but little alarm,—the shops were nearly all open, and as camels and country carts were passing through the streets, it was evident the western and southern gates had been reopened. At the Chinese wall we turned to the eastward, but had not gone far when the street opened into a kind of square, with large buildings on two sides facing each other. On the south side there was a street leading through a large gateway into the Chinese city, and on the north a street which passed under a high archway into the Imperial city. The buildings were those belonging to the principal public departments; they were all large, but appeared to vie with each other in decay and ruin.

We rode a short distance into the Imperial city. The road or street is bounded on either side by high walls, and on looking through the occasional doors and openings which we passed, there appeared to be nothing but a succession of dirty half-empty streets beyond. Within the Imperial city is another walled inclosure, which surrounds the Emperor's palace and gardens and the palaces belonging to the Imperial family.

After going over upwards of a dozen buildings, we selected the Hall of Ceremonies as the place in which to sign the Convention and exchange the Ratification of the Treaty.

We returned by the eastern street, past the Board of Punishments where we had been imprisoned. I had a strong desire to visit it, but on my suggesting through Parkes to do so, the mandarins with us, urged so strongly that we should not go that I did not press the point. We now turned to the north, and as we had as yet failed in securing any suitable house for the Embassy, we visited several on our way, but were unsuccessful. While in a state of uncertainty we saw the roofs of some large buildings about three-quarters of a mile to our right, and Parkes hearing on inquiring that it was a palace belonging to Tsai, the Prince of I,—the Commissioner who had been the prime mover in our capture,—we decided if the accommodation sufficed, to appropriate his house as the residence for the British Embassy. We had been now some hours moving from place to place, and thought it needless to take the escort with us, but suggested to Colonel Ross they should halt and rest, while we went to inspect the buildings; taking with us, therefore, only a Sikh to hold our horses, we cantered to the palace, —the distance was further than we had expected. On arriving at the principal gate, which opened into a fine street, we found it open, and from the appearance of two courtyards through which we passed the whole place was apparently deserted; seeing, however, a good number of buildings beyond, separated from each other by gardens and courtyards, and the doors opening from one to the other being too low to ride through, we dismounted, Parkes saying, as we had no time to spare, if I would explore in one direction, he would in another, and we would soon see if the buildings were suitable for our purposes. Leaving the Sikh holding our horses, we hurried off. I had not gone far when I heard Parkes calling to me, I ran back and met him coming forward; he was excited and exclaimed, "Come here! come here!" and led me through a small door into a large courtyard full of mandarins; pushing past several of whom, we came up to a man whose face I well remembered,—he was the President of the Board of Punishments. " Do you recollect that man?" Parkes asked me. I replied "I do," and that he had been especially brutal in his manner to me. Parkes said, "Ah, and so he was to me;" and then addressing the astonished mandarins in Chinese, he told them that the conduct of this man had been a disgrace to their country, and spoke in the strongest terms of condemnation of the manner in which he had behaved to us. While Parkes was speaking to them in this strain, I looked round and saw we were surrounded, and that they appeared to listen with anything but satisfaction to Parkes' remarks; the manner in which they closed the doors, and their looks generally, made it apparent, that in all probability we would have some further experience of prison life. I therefore said to Parkes, "Take care, or we shall have some difficulty in getting away." At this moment I observed a military mandarin of high rank, who had frequently visited us in the temple, and whose manner had always been civil and considerate, about to leave the court. Pointing him out to Parkes, I asked him to take this opportunity of expressing our thanks for his former courtesy. Parkes at once called to him by name, and said we were glad to be able thus publicly to express our sense of the honourable character of his behaviour, for, said Parkes, even when in misfortune and in prison, he had known how to treat officers with kindness and consideration; that we should be always ready to acknowledge such conduct, and welcome as friends those who acted as he had done; but, continued Parkes, turning to the President of the Board of Punishments, when a man takes advantage of the misfortunes of an enemy, personally to insult him, then he forfeits the consideration of every civilized nation, and deserves to be banished from the society of honest men. The effect of these remarks was wonderful; the faces of all, with the one exception of that of the President of the Board of Punishments, who precipitately retired, brightened, and after a few amiable expressions of good will, we regained our horses, and were glad enough to get back to the escort. We decided, however, to take possession of the buildings for the use of the Embassy, which intention we announced to the Chinese authorities.

Monday, the 22*nd.*—Wade and Parkes busy in the preparation of the Convention. I went with several others to the Prince of I's house to make arrangements for its being prepared for our reception.

The Chinese army, on the advance of the Allies to the north of Pekin, had retired to the west of the city; it had subsequently retreated to a further distance, and was now supposed, greatly reduced in numbers, to be about twelve miles off, near the southwestern suburbs. Reconnoitering parties, under Colonel Probyn and Major Fane, had, at different times, fallen in with their advanced pickets, but no hostile move was attempted on either side.

CHAPTER XVI.

SIGNATURE OF CONVENTION.—RETURN TO ENGLAND.—FUTURE POLICY TO BE PURSUED TOWARDS CHINA.

THE destruction of Yuen-Ming-Yuen, although never referred to by Prince Kung, had been felt, we had reason to know, most acutely by the Chinese authorities as a punishment directed specially against the Emperor and themselves.

The determination of the Allied Commanders-in-Chief to retire into winter quarters at Tien-tsin and Taku, necessitated an early day being fixed for the signature of the Convention ;—the 24th was therefore named for this purpose.

It was unfortunate that the Ambassadors were thus hurried, for it rendered their task of effectually completing their work one of great difficulty. Lord Elgin considered, that even if it could be for only a week, it was very desirable the Embassy should be established in Pekin. Arrangements were therefore hurried forward as rapidly as possible, and there were daily discussions between Messrs. Wade and Parkes and various Chinese deputies, amongst whom were Hang-ki and Hwang.

The mode of ratification had also to be carefully considered, to avoid hereafter any repudiation on the part of the Emperor. It was at last decided that the great Seal of the Empire, and the Emperor's decree authorising Prince Kung to append it, together with a document stating that he was so authorised, sealed and signed by Prince Kung, should be considered a sufficient ratification.

On the forenoon of Wednesday, the 24th, Lord Elgin, accompanied by a large escort, started for the Hall of Ceremonies. He was carried in a chair of state by sixteen Chinamen dressed in royal crimson liveries; the escort consisted of six hundred men, besides one hundred officers. A body of cavalry led, followed by infantry; the officers who had permission to attend came next, the Head-Quarter Staff in rear of them, then the Commander-in-Chief with his Personal Staff, and, about thirty yards behind Sir Hope Grant, came Lord Elgin, his horse saddled and led close behind his chair, the members of the Embassy on either side the Ambassador; a detachment of infantry closed the procession.

Sir Robert Napier, who had charge of the military arrangements, occupied with his division all the important points along the line of route from the An-ting Gate to the Hall of Ceremonies. Crowds of Chinese lined both sides of the streets through which we passed; they were exceedingly quiet and well-behaved, and there was an entire absence of any appearance of alarm. There was immense curiosity, however, to see Lord Elgin; the people pressed forward as his chair passed to obtain a glimpse of a man who at that time was more powerful than even their own Emperor.

The Board of Ceremonies was upwards of three miles from the An-ting Gate, and from the slow pace and occasional halts, the afternoon was well advanced when we arrived there. Dense crowds surrounded the entrance and filled the streets and square; an open passage was kept by our men and by large bodies of the Chinese police. Lord Elgin's personal guard, on entering the courtyard, formed up on either side. The hall selected for the ceremony was quite open on the side facing the court; the officers who accompanied Lord Elgin ranged themselves on the left of the hall, while on the right, opposite, were assembled upwards of a hundred mandarins; at the back were two small tables close together, with one chair at each, fronting the court; the one on the left was for Lord Elgin, the other for Prince Kung. Close to Lord Elgin's there was a chair placed for Sir Hope Grant; along the sides at right angles to these were chairs and tables for the high officers of either nation; behind these, again, were more chairs and tables for the accommodation of the others.

As Lord Elgin's chair entered the gate the bearers, crouching down with bended backs and knees, rushed forward (this being in strict accordance with Chinese etiquette,) to the steps, two or three in number, that led to the hall; the guards presenting arms, and the bands playing "God save the Queen."

Prince Kung advanced to receive Lord Elgin with an anxious, hesitating salutation; Lord Elgin bowed, and at once walked forward to his seat, motioning Prince Kung to take the one on the right. A table stood in the centre of the space formed by the officers and mandarins, and on this the boxes containing the Convention and Treaty were placed. Business commenced by Mr. Wade handing the translation of Lord Elgin's full powers to Prince Kung, who said, although his were not so long as Lord Elgin's they were equally ample. A mandarin of high rank then opened a box that was on the table, and took out some papers wrapped round with yellow silk, which he held with great reverence above his head, and placed before the Prince, who handed them to one of the Ministers of State to read. It was the Emperor's decree conferring on him full powers to negotiate and conclude a peace, and also to affix the great Seal of the Empire to the Treaty, as a proof of its being ratified. The Convention was then signed, and each Plenipotentiary attached his seal to the document;—upon which the Treaties were formally exchanged. A paper was then signed and sealed by Prince Kung, in which he stated that the ratification of the Treaty had been duly executed, and that the great Seal being affixed, meant, that the Emperor accepted all the conditions and clauses in the said Treaty.

A few words were now exchanged between Lord Elgin and Prince Kung, to the effect that they hoped the Convention just signed, and the Treaty which had been ratified, would be the means of establishing a lasting friendship and a good understanding between the two Governments and countries. After a few further remarks, Lord Elgin rose to take leave; Prince Kung accompanied him a short distance, and then stopped; but on Lord Elgin doing so likewise, the principal mandarins in attendance urgently beckoned Prince Kung to move forward, and after a few moments of hesitation he walked with Lord Elgin to the edge of the steps.

Prince Kung at that time was only twenty-eight years of age, but looked older; his countenance is intelligent, but there was an expression of anxious care, which, considering the circumstances of his position, was not unnatural. If he felt fear, he concealed his apprehensions; but the unusual part he was called upon to perform could not fail to be distasteful to his feelings, so contrary as it must have been to any he had been accustomed to act in the presence of the high officers of Government.

There was a curious mixture in the manner of the mandarins towards him,—of great deference accompanied with familiarity. Those who explained the various documents laid before the Prince for his signature, and who assisted in the conversation—if such it can be called that passed between him and Lord Elgin,—while their manner was respectful, spoke with evident freedom, and his tone and manner to them were more that of a friend than of a personage for the time invested with and exercising the royal prerogatives of the Emperor.

The Chinese could not fail to be struck by the quiet, dignified way in which Lord Elgin performed his part in the ceremony. He made it apparent by his manner, that in his opinion signing the Convention and exchanging the ratified Treaties was a benefit conferred on the Chinese Empire rather than any advantage acquired by Great Britain; and Lord Elgin gave the Government clearly to understand, that the recollection of the absence of good faith which had hitherto characterised its proceedings, could only be erased by a strict and sincere regard for the future of treaty obligations.

The grave and serious attention with which the great Princes and Ministers of the Empire watched Lord Elgin's manner, and listened to his remarks, as if thoroughly impressed by the dangerous crisis they were tiding over, but alive to the dangers which still threatened, was one of the most imposing parts of the day's proceedings.

Thus was happily concluded an event which was the commencement of a new era, not only in the history of the Empire of China, but of the world, by the introduction of four hundred millions of the human race into the family of civilized nations.

The French Convention was signed the following day.

Lord Elgin entrusted the conveyance of the Convention and Treaty to my care, and Baron Gros honoured me with the charge of similar documents for the Imperial Government—M. Bastard being unfortunately too ill to perform the journey.

Lord Elgin at one time thought of sending me to England by way of Siberia, but it was afterwards considered the usual route would be the quickest.

Three days after the conclusion of Peace, I started on my homeward journey, bidding an affectionate farewell to the Embassy. On the 27th, I rode to Ho-se-woo, having sent forward horses to Chang-kia-wan; I was delayed some time as my escort, by endeavouring to take a short cut, lost their way, but arriving at Pah-li-chiao bridge, I knew the direction. It was with very different feelings that I now traversed the ground between Tung-chow and Five-li-point which I had passed over so lately; alas! with those whose heroic bearing in all their trials was the sole consolation for their untimely deaths.

Mr. Drake, who commanded a party of Probyn's horse at Ho-se-woo, put me up for the night. I started next morning at daybreak, and changing horses and escort at Yang-tsun arrived at Tien-tsin about noon.

Conveyance of Treaty to England. 291

Major Anson, who was bearer of Sir Hope Grant's despatches, and Colonel Greathed of the Engineers and aide-de-camp to Sir Robert Napier, had preceded me by a day, and I found them on board the "Granada."

The Admiral was at Tien-tsin, and gave me a very kind reception. The following day we started for Taku, where we arrived the same evening. On the morning of the 30th we embarked on board H. M. despatch-vessel "Nimrod," which immediately proceeded to sea. At Shanghai we changed to the regular mail steamer, and after a short detention both at that place and Hong-kong, we arrived in England on 27th December, 1860.

I will add but a few concluding words. Eight years have passed since the events occurred which I have recited. Upon reference to my private Journal, from which I have taken the above extracts, I find written: —"So long as the Chinese governing classes are convinced of our determination and power to punish any breach of faith or departure from the strict rules of justice, and we in our intercourse with them, while respecting their susceptibilities and prejudices, insist with firmness on a due observance of all rights acquired by Treaty ; pursuing, should difficulties arise, the same principle of action that would characterise our conduct in dealing with the great European Powers, I believe the Chinese Government will carry out with loyalty the engagements it has accepted. A knowledge, that can only be acquired by time, of the advantages that will result to themselves from a freer intercourse with European nations, is all that will in future be necessary to induce the Chinese to open the whole Empire to the enterprise of western civilization; but whether such a result is to be attained at an early date, or whether wars, anarchy, and troubles are to precede this period, will mainly depend upon the forbearance exercised by European Powers; there is no country that possesses so great an influence on the future of China as England, or that is so immediately interested in its independence and good government. It should therefore be the policy of this country to support and strengthen the central government at Pekin, and when differences arise, (as they infallibly must from time to time) at points far distant from Pekin, it should be the duty of the British authorities to ignore the independent action of local mandarins, however high their rank, and to look solely for redress at the hands of the Imperial Government. Such a course, should local disturbances break out of a character to threaten and endanger the lives and property of our merchants and countrymen, would not prevent that support and protection being given which it might be in the power of any British force in the immediate neighbourhood to afford; but the Imperial Government, once made to feel that their responsibility was held to extend to the acts of any one of their officials, however distant from the central power the locality might be, would take care to avoid the repetition of such dangers by issuing stringent instructions to the several local authorities that the lives and property of foreign residents were to be respected and regarded."

"From the time Lord Elgin first went to China in 1857, it was his policy to teach the Imperial Government their responsibility in this respect, and on that occasion, as well as on this, by ignoring the Governors-General of those Provinces in which the difficulties which had resulted in war, had first commenced, and making it apparent to the Emperor and his ministers that they were to be held responsible for the acts of their subordinates, he established a principle which, when properly enforced, will do much to lessen in future the danger of similar difficulties occurring, and which on two occasions have involved this country in expensive wars."

In 1862 there was an attempt made, which however fortunately failed, to provide a naval contingent for the service of the Chinese Government, manned and commanded by English officers and men.

The reason that I say "fortunately failed," is that it would have broken through that neutrality which it should be the policy of England to maintain between the Government and the leaders of any rebellion which has, or that may, from time to time arise within the empire of China.

The Chinese mode of suppressing a rebellion is perhaps conducted upon principles which would not always meet with favour if considered from an English point of view, and it would have been difficult to preserve

Future Policy. 295

the English name from being allied with acts the perpetration of which this country would have condemned.

The Chinese generally would have regarded that force, manned by English sailors and officered by gentlemen holding commissions in Her Majesty's Navy, as essentially a part of the British naval forces in those seas; and although the best security for success was taken by placing the Contingent under the command of one of the most able officers in the service, still the fickle goddess, Fortune, cannot always be controlled, and any defeat sustained by the Contingent would have had the same effect on the minds of the Chinese, as if our fleet under the immediate direction of the Admiral had suffered the reverse.

If the Imperial Government of China is ultimately to establish a strong and powerful government throughout the Empire, it must depend on its own exertions, and improve the organization of its military and naval forces; but if it had a European force at its command, on which to rely for the recapture of towns taken by rebels, the Chinese Government would neglect to carry out those measures of administrative reform which are absolutely necessary to enable the Empire to recover from the shocks it has received from foreign wars, and internal disturbances.

Recently the policy which Lord Elgin advocated has been enforced by Lord Clarendon in a manner that cannot fail to lead to good results. In his despatch to Sir Rutherford Alcock, British Minister at Pekin, of the 20th January, 1869, he says: "Her Majesty's Government cannot leave with Her Majesty's Consuls or Naval officers to determine for themselves what redress or reparation for wrong done to British subjects is due, or by what means it shall be enforced. They cannot allow them to determine whether coercion is to be applied by blockade, by reprisals, by landing armed parties, or by acts of even a more hostile character. All such proceedings bear more or less the character of acts of war, and Her Majesty's Government cannot delegate to Her Majesty's servants in foreign countries the power of involving their own country in war."

This is acknowledging, and most properly so, that there is a Chinese as well as an

English point, from which the question should be viewed. Many acts committed by the Chinese local authorities, if properly represented to the Imperial Government, before measures of coercion are adopted, would probably meet with due attention, but so long as the British authority resident in the immediate vicinity of a place where an offence is committed assumes to himself the right of decision as to the nature of the redress to be required, and the persons from whom it is to be demanded, not only will the independent action of the British Minister at Pekin be hampered, but the Imperial Government, however well disposed to remove any reasonable ground of complaint, when urged with moderation and firmness, might from political motives, and from regard for the national honour,—which feeling it should be the policy of England to encourage,—decline to yield, when hostilities had been actually commenced, for the punishment of acts the Government had not been afforded even the opportunity to condemn.

So soon as the Imperial Government is convinced that the responsibility of peace or war is not to rest with irresponsible officers, and that before an appeal is made to war as a last resource, the Government of either Empire will have the opportunity of approving or condemning the acts of its servants, a great step will have been taken towards confirming that degree of confidence in the diplomatic intercourse of the two countries, which it is essential should be maintained, and by which alone England can hope to extend the influence which year by year opens out the resources of China to the enterprise of the world.

THE END.

BRADBURY, EVANS, AND CO., PRINTERS, WHITEFRIARS.

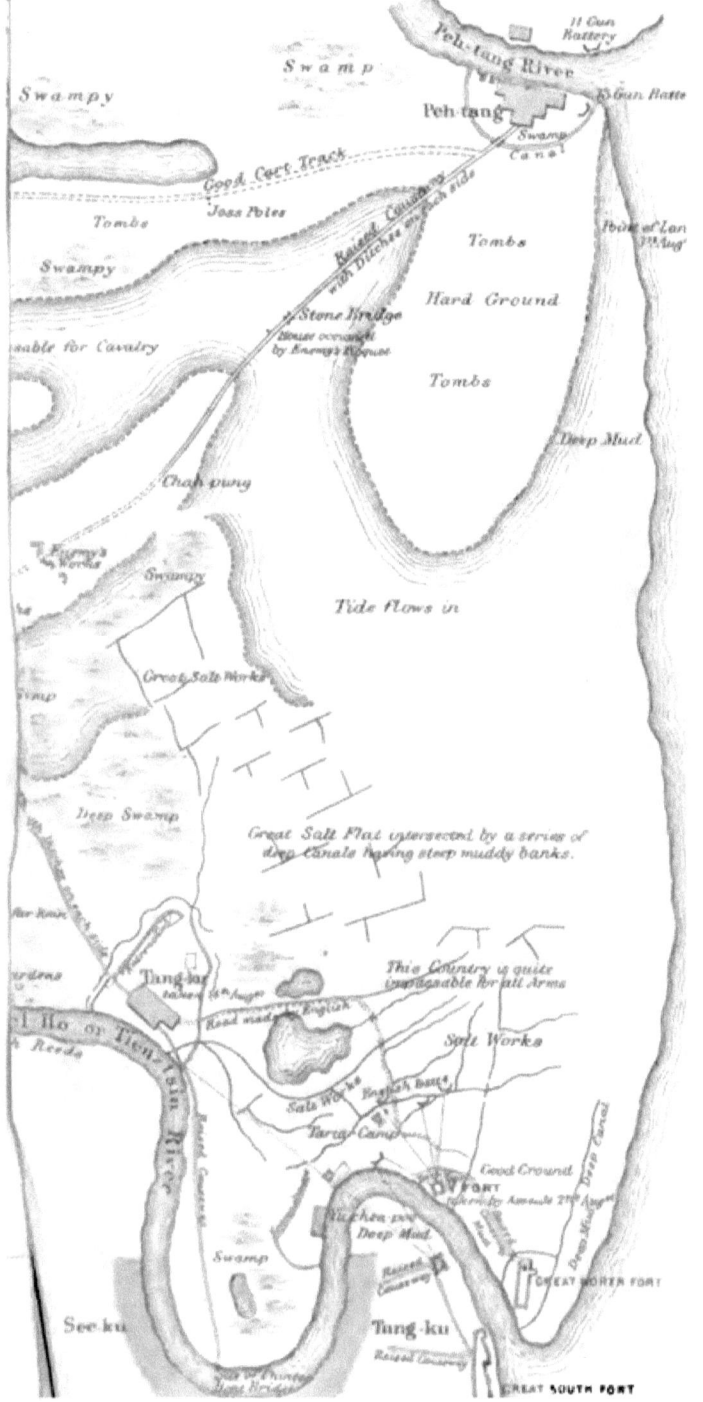

www.ingramcontent.com/pod-product-compliance
Lightning Source LLC
Chambersburg PA
CBHW022053230426
43672CB00008B/1160